What is Politics?

Power, Dissent, Equality: Understanding Contemporary Politics

This book is part of a series produced by Edinburgh University Press in association with The Open University. The complete list of books in the series is as follows:

What is Politics?
Jef Huysmans

Exploring Political Worlds
Edited by Paul Lewis

Politics and Power in the UK
Edited by Richard Heffernan and Grahame Thompson

Living Political Ideas
Edited by Geoff Andrews and Michael Saward

Making Policy, Shaping Lives
Edited by Raia Prokhovnik

The books form part of an Open University course DD203 *Power, Dissent, Equality: Understanding Contemporary Politics.* Details of this and other Open University courses can be obtained from the Course Information and Advice Centre, PO Box 724, The Open University, Milton Keynes MK7 6ZS, United Kingdom: tel. +44 (0)1908 653231, e-mail general-enquiries@open.ac.uk

Alternatively, you may visit the Open University website at http://www.open.ac.uk where you can learn more about the wide range of courses and packs offered at all levels by The Open University.

For availability of other course components visit the webshop at www.ouw.co.uk, or contact Open University Worldwide, Michael Young Building, Walton Hall, Milton Keynes MK7 6AA, United Kingdom for a brochure. tel. +44 (0)1908 858785; fax +44 (0)1908 858787; e-mail ouwenq@open.ac.uk

What is Politics?

Jef Huysmans

Edinburgh University Press
in association with

The Open
University

Edinburgh University Press Ltd
22 George Square, Edinburgh

First published 2005 by Edinburgh University Press Ltd; written and produced by
The Open University

© 2005 The Open University

Edited, designed and typeset by The Open University.

Printed and bound in the United Kingdom by The Alden Group, Oxford.

A CIP record for this book is available from the British Library.

ISBN 0 7486 1966 6 (paperback)

1.1

Contents

The Open University course team

Geoff Andrews, *Staff Tutor in Government and Politics*

Brian Ashcroft, *Associate Lecturer Panel*

Pam Berry, *Compositor*

Karen Bridge, *Media Project Manager*

Vivienne Brown, *Professor of Intellectual History*

Julie Charlesworth, *Lecturer, Open University Business School*

Martin Chiverton, *Media Production Specialist*

Stephen Clift, *Editor*

Lene Connolly, *Print Buyer*

John Craig, *Associate Lecturer Panel*

Michael Dawson, *Course Manager*

Marilyn Denman, *Secretary*

Andrew Dobson, *Professor of Politics*

Lucy Flook, *Course Manager*

Fran Ford, *Course Secretary*

Liz Freeman, *Copublishing Advisor*

Robert Garson, *Reader in American Studies*

Pam Garthwaite, *Course Manager*

Carl Gibbard, *Graphic Designer*

Bram Gieben, *Staff Tutor in Government and Politics*

Janis Gilbert, *Graphic Artist*

Richard Golden, *Production and Presentation Administrator*

Montserrat Guibernau, *Reader in Politics*

Celia Hart, *Picture Researcher*

Richard Heffernan, *Lecturer in Government and Politics*

Wendy Humphreys, *Staff Tutor in Government and Politics*

Jef Huysmans, *Lecturer in Government and Politics*

Bob Kelly, *Staff Tutor in Government and Politics*

Paul Lewis, *Reader in Central and European Politics*

David Middleton, *Staff Tutor in Government and Politics*

Jeremy Mitchell, *Lecturer in Government and Politics*

Raia Prokhovnik, *Senior Lecturer in Government and Politics and Deputy Course Team Chair*

Michael Saward, *Professor in Politics and Course Team Chair*

David Shulman, *BBC Producer*

Lynne Slocombe, *Editor*

Mark J. Smith, *Senior Lecturer in Government and Politics*

Grahame Thompson, *Professor of Political Economy*

Consultant authors

Richard Freeman, *Senior Lecturer in Politics, University of Edinburgh*

Deborah Mabbett, *Lecturer in Politics, Brunel University*

Mads Qvortrup, *Professor of Sociology and Public Policy, The Robert Gordon University, Aberdeen*

Judith Squires, *Senior Lecturer in Politics, University of Bristol*

Nicholas Watson, *Senior Lecturer, School of Health in Social Science, University of Edinburgh*

External assessor

Michael Moran, *Professor of Government, University of Manchester*

Preface

Tumultuous events such as '9-11' and the war and its aftermath in Iraq have reminded people how critical – and sometimes how deadly – the world of politics can be. Even the local, everyday politics of council services, schools and hospitals can affect people's lives powerfully. The Open University, with its unique tradition of interdisciplinary work and its mission to reach and enthuse a hugely diverse student audience, has set out to show why and how politics matters. *What is Politics?* offers a searching but highly accessible entry point to the subject. Building on extended reflections on the case study of asylum seeking in the UK and beyond, it introduces politics by emphasizing its breadth, importance and contested character. It moves away from the narrow and institutional approaches commonly used to introduce politics to undergraduates and general readers. By exploring places and events that are not normally thought of as being 'political', it takes the debate beyond institutions such as the parliament and the national government, and the activities of the political elite. A key goal is to show not simply that politics has an effect on our everyday life but also that our everyday life is itself political. The book uses a case-led approach, drawing general ideas and concepts out of stories, dialogues and press cuttings. It represents an exciting new way to bring politics to life for all readers.

Series preface

This book is one of the five texts which make up the new *Power, Dissent, Equality: Understanding Contemporary Politics* series from The Open University. Each book in the series is designed for students and others who have not studied politics before, and can stand alone as a short introduction to key areas of debate within political science.

Each book offers a distinctive angle on the character and analysis of politics today. *What is Politics?* offers a critical overview, showing the often surprising faces and locations of political life. *Exploring Political Worlds* examines comparative politics, asking what we can learn by looking at one country or context in the light of another. *Politics and Power in the UK* questions how we might make sense of major developments and debates in UK politics, such as devolution and constitutional change. *Living Political Ideas* is an accessible introduction to key topics in political theory and ideology, such as legitimacy, national self-determination, dissent and social justice. *Making Policy, Shaping Lives* teases out and interrogates the many faces of public policy and policy making, drawing on case materials ranging from the single European currency to disability politics.

For all of the books, apart from *What is Politics?*, the chapters follow a common thematic structure. There are five organizing themes. *Powers and structures* explores the meaning and location of power in contemporary societies – what it is, and who has it. *Centre and periphery* looks at issues from the role of the state in our lives to the revival of nationalism in the post-Cold War world. *Participation and dissent* leads us to look, on the one hand, at voting and elections, and on the other hand at new and unconventional forms of political protest and dissent. *Equality and difference* examines how we are seen as 'equal to' and 'different from' each other and how this matters politically. The *evidence and argument* theme focuses attention on the ways in which the study of politics involves both explanation and recommendation.

Courses produced by The Open University are very much a team effort, and *Power, Dissent, Equality: Understanding Contemporary Politics* is no exception. Each member of the course team has made his or her mark on these books, and the work was done with goodwill and good humour. Some special thanks are owed. Raia Prokhovnik's tireless and dedicated contribution as Deputy and Acting Course Chair has been of huge benefit to the course. Mike Dawson has been a superbly calm, tactful and efficient Course Manager. Lucy Flook, Course Manager in the early days, played a significant role in getting the team up and running efficiently and ahead of schedule. Pam Garthwaite kept the momentum going in the period between Lucy's departure and Mike's arrival. The editorial skills of Stephen Clift and Lynne Slocombe and designs by Carl Gibbard have been key to the quality of the texts. Fran Ford has been a great support as course secretary, ably supported at different times by June Ayres and Marilyn Denman. John Craig and Brian Ashcroft have constituted a 'tutor panel' which has commented most helpfully on draft chapters. Robert Garson (Bobby) of Keele University was an influential and insightful member of the course team for two years. Professor Mick Moran of the University of Manchester has been the ideal external examiner – sharp and committed, he has been a tremendously positive influence on the content of these books.

Michael Saward, Course Team Chair

Introduction

[Two people sit in their garden on a sunny summer evening. Marco brings out plates, bread and salad. Michelle pours two glasses of red wine.]

Marco   Busy day at work?

Michelle   The usual stuff. Nothing special. This wine is rather good.

Marco   Is that today's paper?

Michelle   Yep.

Marco   Did you hear that the government wants to introduce an environmental tax?

Michelle   No. I didn't have time to read the paper today ... Marco I've got to tell you something.

Marco   Yes?

Michelle   I'd like to be a student again.

Marco   What? A student! Bit of a backward step isn't it?

   [Silence]

Marco   Okay, why'd you want to study again?

Michelle   I don't know. My brain's going off. I guess I like the idea of playing with knowledge.

Marco   Miss Intellectual!

Michelle   Ha-ha ... But seriously. What do you think?

Marco   Are you going to quit your job?

Michelle   No. I can't afford that. But I could study part time or do a course at The Open University.

Marco   I guess ... What subject are you interested in?

Michelle   Politics. There's so much talk about politics – that it's important, that nobody is interested in it ... I wouldn't mind seeing the wood for the trees when I hear people talking politics.

   [Silence]

Marco   Politics ... politics ... Isn't that a bit boring. Why not study law or economics? Something useful. Or psychology so we can have a bit of fun psycho-analysing one another. But politics ...

Michelle   No I'd rather study politics. People talk a lot about politics but I'm not sure that they, or I for that matter, know what it's about, or what it really is.

   [Silence]

Marco   Okay – so what would you say politics is, Michelle?

Michelle   I guess it's what politicians do.

Marco   And who are politicians?

Michelle   Aren't they a *group of people who do politics* for a living? In the same way that I go to my office and you leave in the morning to finish a flooring job, they do politics for a living.

Marco   Yeh ... But aren't we all supposed to be involved in politics nowadays? Don't we elect our government?

Michelle   But if everyone does politics then there must be something more to politics than what politicians do.

Marco   Maybe politics is what happens in parliaments, local councils, national, regional and local governments, elections ... erm ... political institutions or something.

Michelle   But what about a general strike or an anti-war march? Aren't they political?

Marco   Mmm ... I guess so.

Michelle   Let's try something else.

Marco   What do you suggest?

Michelle   Well, instead of asking who does politics or where it happens, maybe we should look at what politicians do.

Marco   Politicians make policies. That's obvious.

Michelle   But what's a policy?

Marco   Policy making is about deciding who can legally drink alcohol or who can have unemployment benefits. Policies specify tax we have to pay. They can improve access to public transport for disabled people. I guess they also express ideas and values that we consider to be important such as equality and freedom.

Michelle   Hey, I've got it! Do you mean that policies define our rights and duties, that they define what matters for a society? Do politicians not fight for the power to rule a people? It must be quite a task to try to come up with something that makes millions of individuals happy. How do you reconcile people who prefer higher benefits with people who like to pay lower taxes?

Marco   (Smiles) Hmmm, not bad at all! I am impressed. You'll make an excellent student of politics!

Michelle   Yeah, right. But do you know what strikes me as the really critical question: who are the people? Where are the borders of the society? Who is a member of the political community? Are immigrants members? Does Westminster have the power to decide policies for Scotland or Wales? Do the Basques belong to Spain? Are the

Palestinians citizens of Jordan or of Israel? Or, do they belong to the Palestinian nation with a right to their own territory? And even more radically, can politics happen in a factory or a family?

Marco   (Sounds desperate) You can't stop, can you? Can I have the wine please?

Michelle   Come on Marco this is getting interesting. I am pretty excited now. Maybe there is a politics in me pouring the wine and you drinking it. Reminds me of servants and masters (laughs and pours herself another glass of wine). And why are we drinking South African wine while you refused to drink it for years because of the anti-apartheid boycott? Don't you remember? I couldn't see who was being helped by us not buying it.

Marco   Pffff ... Michelle! Don't try to see politics everywhere please. Maybe you shouldn't study politics after all! I still want to enjoy my drink without having to think about the political implications. Can you imagine what a nightmare it'll be to go shopping with you?

Michelle   Oh yes, doing politics while shopping! Brilliant idea! Studying politics is going to be fun.

Marco   No, seriously. Are you sure politics courses deal with all these issues? I thought they focused on how political institutions work and what politicians do. Will they really teach you about wine and shopping?

Michelle   There must be courses that treat politics as a more multidimensional activity than the traditional bits on politicians, elections and institutions. The activity of politicians in the formal political institutions of a country surely is important but political scientists must be aware there's more to politics than that.

Marco   (Finishes his glass) Hey, what about this? We are 'doing politics' here and now by talking about it.

Michelle   (Laughs) Shall we go inside and do some gender politics?

Similar to the conversation between Michelle and Marco, the purpose of this book is to introduce some questions about what makes a wide variety of experiences and events 'political'. It aims to demonstrate the complexity, breadth and importance of politics.

Politics covers many aspects of life. It ranges from national and international issues, such as taxes and war, to local matters, such as maintaining roads and parks. Many people are involved in politics. For example, in discussing how to improve teaching facilities, school governors run into issues of values and authority. People lobbying to maintain conservation areas might face opposition from others wanting to use the area for recreational or economic purposes. Politics can happen anywhere. In supermarkets, for example, consumers can decide not to buy products that contain genetically modified ingredients; or they can decide to ignore calls for boycotting particular products. Politics affects life in a wide variety of ways. A postal strike means that mail is not delivered. Putting extra money into public libraries means that more books, videos and DVDs will be available for borrowing.

By emphasizing the complexity and multidimensional nature of politics this book goes beyond more traditional introductions to politics. The latter tend to focus on the activities of politicians and the main political institutions such as parliament and government. This book emphasizes the importance of looking for politics in unusual places and events to develop an understanding of politics that reflects and casts light on its many faces.

I use five questions to explore a multifaceted understanding of politics:

- Why is politics important?
- Who does politics?
- Where does politics happen?
- Who belongs to a political community?
- How does one encounter the state?

Many places and issues could be examined to illustrate and explore these questions; I look at political refugees as a running example throughout the book. Since the mid 1980s some very emotional debates concerning this issue have been going on in Europe. These debates provide a rich source for exploring both familiar and less familiar aspects of *who has power or authority, why and over what, and how power and authority are enacted and contested.* For example, we will look at how a refugee paying with a voucher in a supermarket relates to politics; we will ask whether decisions by judges on cases related to refugee policy can be political; we will reflect on whether detention centres for refugees are a political place. Refugees raise some tough political questions about who belongs to a political community, the obligations of citizens of a state towards those who are persecuted, and how to properly manage population flows.

Despite the many examples relating to the refugee question, this book should not be mistaken for an introduction to refugee policy. My concern is the notion of politics, in a broader sense. I try to show that there is an unfamiliar face and a familiar face to politics, using examples related to political refugees. I show that politics permeates our everyday experiences. The breadth of politics means it is very difficult to identify precisely what is political and what isn't, and how ready-made black-and-white definitions do not always help. As a consequence, politics may become increasingly unfamiliar and difficult to pin down. I see this as a strength rather than a weakness. To me, formulating a single definition of politics is not a priority – the really important issue is to trigger an interest in reflecting critically and systematically on a wide range of political experiences and phenomena.

Why is politics important?

'Why is politics important?' is a question that invites grand philosophical answers. For example, we might say that human beings are at heart political beings. They differ from animals because they have to create their way of life through struggle, debate, reason and collective decisions rather than by relying on natural instincts. They need to find a common basis for living together. So, politics is important because it is in the nature of human beings to be political. Reflecting on the nature of politics is thus also a reflection on what it means to be a human being.

This chapter, like the rest of the book, does not follow this path of metaphysical reflections. It starts from a more common way of explaining why politics is important. In politics a society shapes what it considers to be important questions for the community. In other words, political activity sets the agenda that contains the important policy questions for a community and its members – that includes you and me – in a particular time. In the late twentieth and early twenty-first centuries refugees were such a question in Western Europe.

As I will show in this chapter, looking at political practice is important. It helps us to understand *why particular phenomena*, such as drugs, refugees or the minimum wage, *are put on the political agenda and thereby made a public issue that bears on a wider community of people*. But it also helps us to understand how politics plays a crucial role in *defining the specific meaning of these particular issues and in changing their meaning over time*. Here, I will use the political definition of an increase in refugee numbers as a 'flood' in the early 1990s as an example of how politics determines how a particular phenomenon is understood.

Let's go back in time to the autumn of 1989.

The autumn of 1989 was an exciting time in Europe. It marked the beginning of the end of the international politics of the second half of the twentieth century. After the Second World War, Europe was split into two camps: a communist East and a liberal-democratic West. Each was led by a superpower: the Soviet Union and the United States of America. The two superpowers and their allies were in conflict but without directly engaging one another in war. The Cold War between the two superpowers held the world in its grip for more than 40 years. During that time walls and fences were erected to separate the two blocs from one another. The Iron Curtain, which stretched from Szczecin in the Baltic to Trieste in the Adriatic, and the Berlin Wall, which separated East Berlin from West Berlin, prevented information exchange and free movement between Eastern and Western Europe.

In 1989 things changed dramatically. The German embassies in Prague and Budapest were overrun by people from Eastern Europe wanting to escape to Germany. Others were cutting holes in the Iron Curtain. The symbolic moment signifying the end of an era was the fall of the Berlin Wall. Later, in 1991, the Soviet Union fell apart. At that point, the Cold War was

FIGURE 1   Berlin, 1961: West Berliners watching over the wall to the East

really over and a new era dawned. Europe was no longer split into two military and ideologically opposed blocs.

Celebrations went hand in hand with claims of victory. The 'free world' had finally defeated communism. Some even went as far as saying that history had ended: there would be no real challenges to a world of democracy and free markets any more. However, worries that many Central and Eastern Europeans would migrate to Western Europe soon dampened the celebrations of unity and rediscovered freedom in the West. A Polish citizen fleeing to West Germany would have been welcomed with open arms in the early 1980s. Within a year after the Iron Curtain had disappeared, the same citizen would be perceived as a burden. West European countries preferred that East Europeans stayed in their own countries.

For that purpose, some commentators argued, West European countries erected a new wall. Like the old wall, it was designed to keep people in Central and Eastern Europe. However, this time it was patrolled on the Western rather than the Eastern side. Let's have a look at two quotations, one from November and

FIGURE 2   Berlin, November 1989: East Germans move through the dismantled wall into West Berlin

another from September 1990. Both illustrate the shift from celebrating the end of the Cold War to new worries about refugees and immigrants. These worries played a role in making refugees and immigrants a prominent political issue in the 1990s.

Driving from Vienna to Czechoslovakia or Hungary is immeasurably easier now than it was even one month ago. British visitors, like most other West Europeans, can pass through easily, visas no longer required. The Common European Home in action. But you soon realize that the rules are not the same for everyone, and certainly not for the traffic in the other direction. In the borderlands, exactly a year after the Berlin Wall was breached, there are scenes more reminiscent of the US–Mexico boundary – armed Austrian troops on patrol to keep the eastern aliens out. In Brussels, the Eurocrats are having shudders as they wonder what to do about the huddled masses of the late 20th century – the 'illegals' from the East who are knocking on the door. Freedom of movement, that sine qua non [indispensable condition] of the European Community, has its limit. The limit is the old Iron Curtain, which, it turns out, has not been completely dismantled ...

(Traynor, 1990, p.21)

About 2,000 Austrian soldiers were sent to the Hungarian border yesterday to halt a flood of refugees from Eastern Europe. A year ago, Austrians welcomed tens of thousands of East Germans who fled over the newly-opened Iron Curtain frontier. They quickly left the country and travelled to West Germany. The soldiers' task is to prevent the illegal entry of East Europeans, mainly Romanians, seeking the 'Golden West' and above all jobs. The soldiers were reinforcing Customs guards who could no longer stem the tide, running at more than 100 people daily. Austrian refugee camps are overflowing with 20,000 asylum seekers, 13,000 of them Romanians. Thousands more are living illegally in Austria and other Western countries are not interested in accepting them.

(Hoffer, 1990, p.12)

FIGURE 3   The border between Germany and Poland, June 1993: a family of clandestine immigrants is captured by customs officers

Soldiers patrolling the border to keep refugees out of Western Europe! This might sound quite familiar in the twenty-first century. After all, immigrants and refugees have been very visible on the political agenda and in the media for a while now. One gets used to particular images and policies, such as the Italian border police chasing Albanians in the Adriatic. But try to relocate yourself in the watershed of 1989 and the celebrations of the end of the Cold War. The image of the new wall is a very strong one that indicates a dramatic shift in political perception of Central and Eastern Europeans. The following quotation by Ismail Kadare, which pictures migration as the mother of war, gives a sense of some of the dramatic imagery that went hand in hand with the shift in policies.

In the past thousand years, Albania has suffered two tragic waves of emigration. The first was in the 15th century, the second in 1990–1991, both to Italy and both by sea. The first was caused by the Ottoman invasion, at its beginning; the second, by communist dictatorship, at its end. The first wave was made up of the elite of the country: lords, bishops, officers, who left with their luggage, their records, and even their church bells, which they didn't want to leave to the Turks. The second was made up of simple people, most of them jobless, with no belongings, sometimes just wearing their sandals. The first were received as heroes, given land and villages where they could settle, invited to celebrate mass and join in local ceremonies. The second were stuffed into barracks and given plastic bags, of the kind used to cover corpses, to protect them from the cold. The migrations which heralded the end of communism were only a prologue to the movement of individuals, groups, and entire peoples which could occur in the future. We stand on the brink of a period of new migrations. Should we fear them? I think so. Our minds, accustomed to the routine of things, imagine dangers in a static form, but dangers can also change shape. Migration of large human masses contains the danger of war. In fact, it has been the mother of war.

(Kadare, 1991, p.21)

Although this image of war is much stronger than how the migration and refugee question was usually represented, Kadare nevertheless seems to have articulated the shift in political and popular perception of immigration and refugees in the early 1990s quite well.

Throughout the 1990s, immigration and, especially, refugees became increasingly negatively portrayed as a burden and many policy initiatives were developed to keep unwanted immigrants and refugees out of Western European countries. Refugees and immigrants did become a very hot issue in domestic public debates. Opinions polarized and refugees often made the headlines. Let's look at the United Kingdom ten years later. Two short extracts from newspaper articles are sufficient to indicate the prominence of the refugee issue in domestic politics in the UK.

The Catholic bishops of England and Wales came close to urging their parishioners not to vote for William Hague yesterday as they issued their strongest attack yet on politicians of all parties for stirring up social divisions over asylum seekers. In a statement after a meeting in London, they accused politicians and some in the media of damaging community relations and giving rise to hostility and fear by attacks on refugees.

(Bates, 2000, p.6)

Thousands of asylum seekers are to be dumped in villages already plagued by the menace of rural crime, it was revealed yesterday. The refugees will join the rising numbers of criminals and drug addicts living in country communities on various rehabilitation programmes. It is part of Jack Straw's plan to move asylum seekers away from London and the south east, areas which have taken the brunt of the backlog of the 90,000 people and their families who are claiming refugee status. The towns and villages of the south west seem set to be the new target for the influx of immigrants. Yesterday, it was revealed a third refugee centre has been planned for Somerset. It means up to 5,000 refugees could flood into the West Country by next April even though accommodation is secured for only 250.

(Clarke, 2000, p.31)

Barriers go up against human tide

NEW Iron Curtain is ... ... on Europe from ... to the shores of the ... ... But the ... frontier of the ... ... is noth- ... This

Hundreds of thousands of ref... the rich and the poor. I...

...ting to cross Europe's yawning gulf between ... measures being taken to stop them

EU must halt refugee flood

...overnments are to ... Britain's refugee

Gypsies flood into Britain in asylum quest

by Stephen ...

Crisis as Colombian refugees flood into Britain

The flood of asylum seekers hits record

RECORD numbers are claiming political asylum in Britain, according to official Home Office figures obtained by the Daily Mail.

More than 43,000 took refuge here last year, the report reveals. That is 11,000 more than 1994 and nearly double the figure for 1993.

The dramatic increase, which is the second highest rise in Europe, comes ...

By DAVID WILLIAMS
Chief Reporter

political asylum once they were settled in Britain either illegally or on visitors' visas. Half of those put in their applica- tions when arrested or in connection with criminal offences. Only ... per cent are likely to ...

A contro...

fears of those, like Home Secretary Michael Howard, who believe Britain is being deliberately targeted because it has become a 'soft touch'.

'Those fears will be given further ... by a statistic ...

Ian Burrell

rampage. More than 100 police officers, many in riot gear, were

FIGURE 4   The portrayal of immigration and refugees. Clockwise from top: *The Herald*, October 1995; *Sunday Times*, October 1997; *The Independent*, August 1997; *Daily Mail*, January 1996; *News of the World*, October 1999

Headlines articulating theatrical language similar to Kadare's, bishops almost urging people not to vote for a particular party, worries about refugees and crime, worries about the implications of the negative portrayal of refugees for racial policies ... . At the dawning of the twenty-first century fierce and polarized public debates about the free movement of people still continue.

The story I have told so far about refugees and the way in which they are portrayed triggers a number of questions. How did refugees become such a prominent political question? Why did moving from East to West change, almost overnight, from something to be celebrated into a danger? Did the people change? Did the numbers increase? Can an increase in numbers explain such a dramatic shift in tone? How can it be explained that limiting population flows into Western European countries stayed a political priority after it became clear that the flood of Central and Eastern Europeans which one expected did not materialize? Most answers to these questions would inevitably highlight the importance of political activity in placing the refugee question on the political agenda and in shaping the perception of the refugee question. Let's try to hint at the significance of politics and the complexity of agenda setting by reflecting, for a brief moment, on one of the most common answers to the question 'Why did refugees become a political problem?': the increase in numbers of asylum applications and of refugees arriving in Western Europe.

Table 1 shows the number of asylum applications in the UK between 1980 and 1999.

TABLE I   Asylum applications in the United Kingdom, 1980–99

1980	1981	1982	1983	1984	1985	1986	1987	1988	1989	Total
2352	2424	4223	4296	4171	4389	4266	4256	3998	11,640	46,015

1990	1991	1992	1993	1994	1995	1996	1997	1998	1999	Total
26,205	44,840	24,605	22,370	32,830	43,965	29,640	32,500	46,015	71,145	374,115

Source: UNHCR, 2001

Undoubtedly, these data, taken from a report published by the Population Data Unit of the United Nations High Commissioner for Refugees, show that the number of asylum applications submitted in the UK did significantly increase in the 1990s. On average, the UK received 4601 asylum applications every year between 1980 and 1989. This average went up to 37,411 applications between 1990 and 1999 (UNHCR, 2001, pp.145, 155).

What do such numbers tell us? In a sense the evidence of a rising number of refugees does not tell us anything that is politically significant. It just indicates that on average there are more applications for asylum in the 1990s than in the 1980s. Why would this increase in numbers be important for a society of over 50 million people? The refugee population in Kenya, with a total population of approximately 29 million, was 402,200 in 1992 and went down to 223,700 in 1999, for example. In the UK, the number went up from 47,100 in 1992 to 93,100 in 1999 (UNHCR, 2002). Does this mean that refugees are a bigger problem for the UK than for Kenya because in the UK the numbers doubled while in Kenya they fell back to half the number of 1992? Or, should we rather look at the total number of refugees which in Kenya is still more than double the number in the UK in 1999? Or, should we look at the total number of refugees in proportion to total population: 0.77 per cent for Kenya, 0.19 per cent for the UK in 1999? (You may have noticed that there is a difference between the figures in Table 1 from the UNHCR report and the figures from the second UNHCR source, the *Statistical Yearbook 2001*. One of the reasons may be that not all refugees apply for asylum or enter the asylum statistics. There may be a variety of other explanations too. The point is that if one argues with and about numbers it is important to check what the numbers count and how they have been compiled.)

Without arguments explaining why the increase in refugees is important for the UK, the evidence is politically not very interesting. Moreover, there is no evidence that the increase in refugees necessarily adds up to something we might call a 'flood'. For example, a few hundred Slovakian Roma Gypsies triggered a national outburst in October 1997 while a year and a half later more than 10,000 asylum applications from the former Federal Republic of Yugoslavia (FRY) (renamed Serbia and Montenegro in February 2003) did not. Clearly, the numbers do not tell the whole story. They do not give us an idea of the motives of refugees, of reactions of the public in the UK or of policies the government has developed. Most importantly, they do not explain by themselves why a few hundred Roma refugees constitute a 'flood' and 10,000 refugees from the FRY do not.

To help illustrate these points, try the following. If you look at the numbers in Table I without any other information available, how would you answer the question 'What do these figures tell us about refugees?' Would you be able to come up with an answer that says more than 'well, it seems that the numbers have gone up'? Would you think the figures for the 1990s signal a flood? Or, do you lack information that would allow you to say whether they represent a flood or not?

The conclusion to this short reflection on numbers seems to be that the interesting questions do not follow from the numbers as such but from what they are made to mean. To create a political stake the evidence of the numbers has to be integrated into a political argument. One of the successful arguments was that the rise in refugees, as evidenced in the statistics, created a dangerous flood that seriously challenged UK society and its achievements. Others contested this interpretation. As a result, a statistical figure turns into an issue of national debate about what is good for UK society.

Arguments and ideas that are capable of linking refugees to a more general question for a political community are the ones that can make refugees politically significant. Without introducing political ideas, these refugees remain, for example, a subject of demographic observation or a curiosity, but not a political issue.

Thus politics is not simply about putting issues on or keeping them off the political agenda. Putting refugees on the political agenda is closely intertwined with arguing what 37,411 applications for asylum mean for a country and its people. Consequently, if one wants to understand why refugees – or any other issue for that matter – are perceived as a problem for the UK, Germany, the USA, or any other country, one has to look at the political processes that have turned the increase in the number of asylum applications into a question of national significance.

In this process the language one uses to describe phenomena is important. It determines to an extent how a policy question is approached. The language of 'a flood of Roma' compared with the language of 'compassion for victims of the war in Kosovo' implies a different understanding and ultimately also a different treatment of refugees. Since the language one uses is so important, it is not surprising that contesting the language that is being used and proposing alternative understandings of a policy question is a substantial part of politics. In other words, politics is always also a politics of language.

These observations lead us back to the question of why politics is important. It is in and through political practice that the life of refugees becomes meaningful and of significance to the national state, its regions and its citizens. Political arguments deal with questions about whether there are too many refugees or not, whether refugees are a burden or whether they make a positive contribution to society, and whether refugees should be removed from a country or whether a country has an international obligation to protect refugees. Political arguments define whether, how and why an increase in the number of refugees is important for a society. In other words, politics sets the agenda. It is a contest of appropriate definitions of the refugee question on the basis of which policies are developed and contested.

Of course, this is not confined to the refugee question. Many issues that affect our everyday lives are also defined, shaped and changed on the basis of particular understandings – or, in other words, specific politicizations – of a problem. For example, the reform of public health services, the privatization of national railways, opening hours of pubs, state-funded childcare, and laws against racial discrimination and xenophobia undergo similar processes, shifting and shaping the meaning of phenomena and in doing so their political significance.

Now let's try a variation on the previous exercise. This time do not clear your mind at all. Look at the statistics on asylum applications or refugees from the UNHCR for a country of your choice. The section on statistics of the UNHCR website (http://www.unhcr.ch/cgi-bin/texis/vtx/statistics) has several reports, including the statistical yearbooks. Now answer the same question, 'What do these figures tell us about refugees?' Look at your answer and try to reflect on how your understanding of the data has been shaped by the political debates and refugee policies in your country. Which parts of your answer refer to political arguments you are familiar with? Where did you get the knowledge about refugees from?

SUMMARY

Why is politics important?

The usual answer is that it affects you. It creates chances and obstacles in life. For example, subsidized childcare usually implies that women mostly can continue working when they have children. Introducing fees for universities probably reduces the chances that people with lower incomes will encourage their children to go to university. I am sure you can come up with many examples along these lines yourself.

In this chapter, I offered a different angle on how politics affects you. I supported the idea that politics involves disputing existing ways of defining a problem and offering better ways of dealing with it. That means that politics does not simply influence opportunities for you and the refugees but that it also affects what refugees mean to you, how you will relate to them and how they will relate to you. You will most likely relate differently to a victim of torture than to someone who tries to benefit illegally from your taxes, for example. It is not difficult to find other examples. Are universities institutions in which the elite of a society are reproduced or are they institutions that benefit everyone? Is the primary role of women to nurture children and husband, or should they be encouraged to have careers and compete with men in the labour market? These are not just questions about opportunities for lower-income families or women, but about what a good society is and what it means to be a woman.

Thus, politics is important not only because it has an impact on your chances in life but also because it influences and changes how you define yourself, your society and your relation to other people.

Who does politics?

One of the key questions that immediately follows from the previous chapter is this: 'If the numbers do not speak for themselves, who then speaks for the numbers?' Who makes an average of 37,411 refugees per year between 1990 and 1999 (Table 1) stand for a 'flood' of foreigners into the UK? Who has the power to shape what 37,411 refugees means for the UK? Is it the media? Politicians? International organizations? The European Union? Local governments? Skinheads in Dover? The Refugee Council? You?

In this chapter I start from the understanding that politicians mainly define what politics is. In other words, I answer the question 'What is politics?' by referring to the practice of a particular group of professionals: politicians. Subsequently, this answer will be questioned. First, I question this notion of politics by introducing another powerful professional group that may compete with politicians in the authoritative allocation of values and definitions of what is right and wrong for a society: the judges. By means of a few examples I demonstrate that although judges are not politicians their judgements can be an important part of political life. Second, I render the understanding of politics more complex by introducing citizens. Politicians not only compete with and relate to other professional groups but they are also constrained and responsive to questions and activities of citizens, or, in more general terms, the people. Examples will be taken from political processes related to the definition and regulation of refugees.

Let's start with an international example:

> in the aftermath of World War II ... millions of uprooted peoples wandered hungry and aimlessly through devastated landscapes and cities. In a spirit of empathy and humanitarianism, and with a hope that such widespread suffering might be averted in the future, nations came together in the stately Swiss city of Geneva and codified binding, international standards for the treatment of refugees and the obligations of countries towards them.
>
> (Achiron, 2003)

This meeting resulted in the signing of the 1951 Convention relating to the Status of Refugees. The Convention is a major international legal instrument for refugee protection. It defines a refugee as a person who 'owing to well-founded fear of being persecuted for reasons of race, religion, nationality, membership of a particular social group or political opinion, is outside the country of his nationality and is unable, or owing to such fear, is unwilling to avail himself of the protection of that country' (UN Convention relating to the Status of Refugees, 1951, Article 1).

The Convention was not simply a result of empathy and humanitarianism. It was an outcome of tough negotiations between governments. Political leaders, diplomats and their technical advisers bickered over the exact definition of who is a refugee. They fought at length over the Convention's key provision for the protection of refugees: the obligation of *non-refoulement* of refugees, that is the obligation for governments not to expel or return (*refouler*) an asylum seeker to a territory where he or she faces persecution. Diplomats

FIGURE 5   Signing of the 1951 Convention relating to the Status of Refugees

questioned whether non-refoulement applied to persons who had not yet entered a country and, thus, whether governments were under any obligation to allow large numbers of persons claiming refugee status to cross their frontiers' (Achiron, 2003).

Fifty years later West European governments are increasingly pushing for the Convention to be renegotiated. They argue that the refugee problem has significantly changed and that their asylum systems based on the Convention can no longer cope with the flow of asylum seekers. (Asylum is not the same as *non-refoulement*, although there is a close relation between the two. Asylum refers to 'admission of residence and lasting protection against the jurisdiction of another State'; Goodwin-Gill, 1996, p.174. It usually implies more than simply not returning refugees. The practical provisions of asylum are decided nationally but often imply granting residence, work permits, etc. While the Convention contains an obligation of *non-refoulement* it does not contain an obligation of asylum for states and, thus, neither a right of asylum for refugees.)

The UK Prime Minister, Tony Blair, stated in 2001 (quoted in Achiron, 2003; see also Blair, 2001) that although the Convention's values are timeless 'with vastly increasing economic migration around the world and most especially in Europe, there is an obvious need to set proper rules and procedures ... . The United Kingdom is taking the lead in arguing for reform, not of the Convention's values, but of how it operates.' The year before, in April 2000, the then UK Conservative Party leader, William Hague, questioned the convention on similar grounds:

> Throughout Western Europe, the asylum system has proved a soft target for people trying to get round the usual immigration controls. Because the 1951 Convention imposes on each government a duty to assess every application on its merits, a claim for asylum has proved an effective way to gain temporary entry to another country and then to delay or avoid removal or deportation.
>
> (Hague, 2000)

Here we are not primarily interested in different arguments for changing the Convention or in evaluating the claims and assumptions on which they are based. The theme I want to highlight is that this story presents politics to us in a fairly familiar way. Politicians debate a problem. Governments design solutions and thus allocate values, such as the protection of the individual against persecution. If there is enough support for a particular definition of the problem and a way of remedying it, they draw up a piece of legislation – in this case international law – and send it to the parliament for discussion and ratification. Politicians are the key political actors who have the power to make (international) law and, thus, refugee policy. Politicians debated the significance of the refugee situation in Europe after the Second World War and again after the end of the Cold War. Politicians negotiate and bargain about how to deal with the refugee question today. For example, they argue about whether the number of refugees is too high for the present asylum system or whether economic immigrants claiming asylum are abusing the Convention. This image of politics being an activity of professional politicians is very familiar. Many people in Western Europe today would probably think of politics in this way.

However, are politicians really at the heart of politics? Do they really have the highest authority to decide what is right and wrong for a community as a whole? Let's see if I can find some examples of situations in which politicians find themselves caught out by non-politicians in debates about how to deal with the refugee question.

A good source for examples is the outspoken interventions of judges in asylum policy in the UK at the turn of the century.

March 2001:

> The [political] parties are vying with each other to see who can take the toughest line on asylum. But how far will the judges let them go? Just the day before Hague's speech (leader of the Conservative Party), three appeal court judges ... told Jack Straw, the home secretary, that he and the previous Tory home secretary, Michael Howard, had acted irrationally and unlawfully in placing and keeping Pakistan on the (since abolished) white list of safe countries.
>
> (Dyer, 2001, p.48)

December 2001:

> The Home Secretary, David Blunkett, last night renewed his fury at a high court judge who ruled under the Human Rights Act that the policy of fining lorry drivers £2000 for each clandestine stowaway found in their vehicles was unlawful and amounted to 'legislative overkill'.
>
> (Travis, 2001a)

These are two examples of judges overturning political decisions that were aimed at reducing the number of asylum applications in the UK. In the first example, judges decided that calling Pakistan a safe country, which implies that Pakistani refugees could be sent back without considering their individual asylum applications, was not a rational and lawful policy measure. In the second example, a judge decided that fining lorry drivers £2000 for each illegal immigrant who is found in their truck is not compatible with the right to a fair trial (under Article 6 of the European Convention on Human Rights).

The Home Office reacted to the latter decision by saying that the judgement risked the national security of the UK.

> 'Once again the courts have intervened with an interpretation that fails to take account of the reason for the implementation of the policy', said a Home Office spokesman. 'Should an appeal be unsuccessful, the Government would clearly have to indicate an alternative way of holding to account those who brought clandestine immigrants into the country and by doing so in the present circumstances, placed this nation at risk.
>
> (quoted in Johnston, 2001)

On the one hand, we could ask why the Home Office was making such a fuss about the judge's decision in this case. Are judges not the professionals who apply the law? Do they not, together with the parliament, guarantee that some

FIGURE 6 At the heart of politics?: politicians in the House of Commons, judges in the courtroom

of the fundamental principles of democracy are not changed at random by the government? Surely politicians are not above the law? On the other hand, we can also see that there was a conflict of opinion with regard to what kind of instruments one can effectively use to reduce the number of refugees applying for asylum in the UK. Moreover, the Home Office suggested that there was a serious conflict of opinion between the judge and itself on what was at stake for the UK in the debate about controlling the inflow of refugees. The judge prioritized the law and a fair treatment of lorry drivers while the Home Secretary emphasized that national security was at stake and should be given priority, especially in the wake of the terrorist attack on the twin towers in New York (11 September 2001).

I do not want to dwell on this conflict of opinions here. What the story illustrates is that politicians are not the only group of professionals who make decisions about how a society should deal with the refugee question. The decision of the judges, although they are first of all judicial decisions, can be seen as interventions in the debate about both what is at stake in the refugee question and how to deal effectively with the flow of refugees. In that sense, the judges were political actors who actively participated in constructing the UK's way of dealing with the refugee question at the turn of the twentieth century.

However, surely judges are not politicians? In Western democracies merging the function of politician and judge is highly contentious, to say the least. The judicial system has to be largely independent of the political system so as to guarantee that the law can be applied independently of political considerations. Separating judicial power from political power is one of the historical achievements of Western democracies. In part, this separation is designed to prevent politicians considering themselves to be above the law and to guarantee the political neutrality of the judiciary. However, it also introduced two competing authorities, and both have the capacity to define and interpret rights and duties for a community as a whole. In that sense judicial decisions are not apolitical. Despite the fact that acting judges (usually) are not politicians, their decisions can have a political character. As in the examples, judicial decisions can express a serious conflict of opinion between judges and politicians. Such a conflict of opinion matters because both judges and politicians (in the example, the Home Secretary) have authoritative positions in society. Both professions can significantly influence the making and application of policies and thus the shaping of lives of both the refugees and the citizens of a state.

The story of the judges' decisions renders the smooth picture of politicians debating and deciding political issues – with which we started this chapter – more complex. It also emphasizes that politics involves contesting opinions and policies. Adding professional groups, including politicians, judges and civil servants, with the authority to propose, shape, decide and implement policies within the limits of the rule of law introduces a more multifaceted picture of negotiations and competition.

At this point some of you might want to say: 'That is all fine and well but where are the people in all of this? Do the people not participate in politics? Does the authority to make policies in democracies not ultimately depend on consent by the people?' These are very good questions indeed. They clarify that the analysis above presents an elitist understanding of politics. The contestation of political opinion and of policies mainly happens between professional elites. This view obscures one of the cornerstones of democratic rule: rule by the people. Democracy implies that politics also includes the participation of ordinary people. In democracies the policies that the political elite formulates are at least to some extent dependent on the will of the people.

Let's look at a section from 'Common sense on asylum seekers', a speech delivered by William Hague, who was then the leader of the Conservative Party, in April 2000.

> We believe Britain has a moral as well as a legal duty to welcome here people who are fleeing for their lives. That duty includes providing them with decent accommodation, treating them if they fall ill, ensuring that their children have a proper education, giving them the freedom to accept work and the right to family reunion in this country. I believe that if the British people have confidence that they are helping those who have been genuinely dispossessed, they will accept that duty with cheerfulness and generosity.
>
> For that tradition of welcoming refugees to be maintained it needs to continue to command general public support. That *public support* will only be forthcoming if the asylum system is clearly able to distinguish between genuine and unfounded claims, and if it is able to give practical effect to that distinction.
>
> (Hague, 2000, emphasis added)

This statement raises a number of important issues with regard to the refugee question, including moral and legal duties of a state, the distinction between genuine and unfounded asylum claims, and welfare support for asylum seekers. However, for this chapter the more important issue is that it indicates that public support is a key political factor in the development of refugee policy. The speech seems to suggest that without public support, moral and legal duties to protect people fleeing for their lives would be difficult to sustain politically. In that sense, the statement illustrates the common understanding that the opinion of the people on refugees influences, and possibly determines, the opinion of politicians.

But does public opinion play a decisive role in politics? Can the participation of people in politics be understood as the influence of public opinion? Let's look at these questions by unpacking a public opinion poll on attitudes towards migration. An opinion poll is of course not the same as public opinion, but it is a particular way – often sponsored by certain interest groups and/or carefully timed – of registering public opinion.

FIGURE 7 Delacroix, *Liberty Leading the People* (1830): a classic image of popular sovereignty

A *Guardian*/ICM poll taken in May 2001 concluded that 51 per cent of people supported opening doors to people with skills that are not in short supply and unskilled economic immigrants on a quota basis. This figure was seen to oppose the conventional political wisdom that UK citizens were against further immigration or, in other words, 'that there are no votes in being seen to encourage immigration' (Travis, 2001b, p.13). However, 41 per cent of the respondents opposed immigration on a quota basis and 8 per cent did not know. This may indicate that a majority of people supported further immigration under certain conditions. The poll also concluded that 'the majority of people, 56%, do not think any of the parties have a good policy on asylum' (Travis, 2001b, p.14).

Like all public opinion polls this one demonstrated that there is no national consensus. People had and still have different opinions on the refugee question. This raises a few interesting questions about politicians claiming that their policies represent the opinion of the people. How much public support do politicians require? Are all opinions equally important and is the question of public support therefore just a question of a majority opinion? Or, are some opinions more important than others? If so, which section of the public do politicians consider to be more important? Or, in other words, whose opinion will make a difference? For example, does the opinion of 2500 inhabitants of Sully, a village 10 miles outside Cardiff, make a

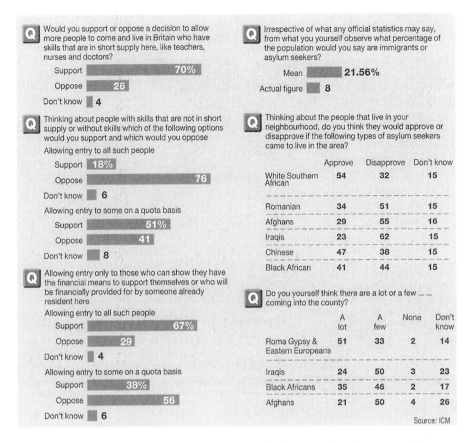

FIGURE 8   A *Guardian*/ICM opinion poll on attitudes towards asylum and refugees
Source: Travis, 2001b, p.14

difference when they protest against a plan to construct a self-contained centre for 750 asylum seekers near their village? Why would the Home Office change a policy decision when a few thousand people protest? In other words, how can expressions of opinion in the periphery influence policy making in the centre? Perhaps when the local politicians lean on the government? When violent protest is used to counter the policy decision by the centre? When opinions are expressed in opinion polls? Why would the opinion of the people from Sully be more important than the opinion of people in another village that would have to house the 750 asylum seekers if the refugee centre was not built in Sully?

These questions indicate that the idea of public support, and thus the relation between the people and the political elite, is more complex than measuring expressions of public opinion.

One way of bringing out the multifaceted nature of this relation is to change the question from 'How much public support does a policy have?' to 'How do people participate in and dissent from political decisions?' The latter question shifts the perspective from measuring opinion to the instruments and strategies

FIGURE 9   Protests in support of and against asylum seekers

for expressing opinions and influencing political agendas. Organizing and participating in opinion polls is obviously one of the possible political instruments to express public support or dissent. But some people would argue that it is more powerful to participate in social movements, unions and business groups than limiting oneself to voting or public opinion polls. Unions and business groups, for example, may have more direct and continuous access to politicians.

In addition, not all opinions are equally important. For example, can people in the periphery influence policy making in the centre? Finally, there is the more provocative question of how the political elite shape and possibly manipulate the opinion of the people. Do people develop political opinions by themselves and by talking to friends? Or, do politicians considerably influence what kind of opinions people will have? If the meaning of an increase in numbers of refugees is created through political argument, as I suggested in the previous chapter, and if politicians – like other professionals such as journalists, civil servants and judges – have privileged access to national public debates, then it is not unrealistic to assume that politicians have an important influence on the kind of opinions that people develop.

Who do you think shapes the refugee question? Who decides what to do? Is it politicians? Judges? The unions? The media? Refugees protesting? Those throwing petrol bombs at refugee centres?

I hope you can see that these issues indicate that the relation between the people and the political elite is multifaceted. The simple notion of 'public support for policies' implies a number of complex questions about political participation and dissent which go beyond the influence of public opinion polls and elections.

At this point, I guess some of you will say: 'This all seems fine, but do these brief reflections actually answer the question of who does politics?' I would answer with a diplomatic yes and no. This chapter indicates that the question is actually a complex one and that this is not surprising given the multifaceted nature of modern politics. Politics cannot be understood by referring to one particular political class – the politicians. Modern politics does involve a variety of actors who are related in multiple ways. In this chapter I developed one way of bringing out the richness of modern politics. I presented politics as being simultaneously a competition among authoritative professional groups in the allocation of values for a community as a whole and the relation between these authoritative groups and the citizens who are members of that community.

However, you would be right if you thought that this picture does not really provide a conclusive answer to the question 'Who does politics?' It does not provide a full list of who count as political actors and of the relationship between them. (For example, I have not included the news media who are definitely important in politics.) Maybe such an answer is not desirable and maybe, ultimately, not a problem either. Perhaps defining who is a significant political actor is necessarily a political matter in itself because it ascribes authority to particular groups of people and, more importantly, not to other groups of people. If this is the case then perhaps it is part of a democratic understanding of politics that one can have contesting understandings of who

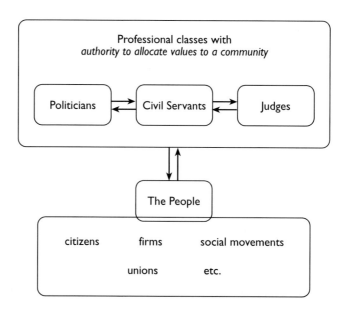

FIGURE 10   Who does politics?

is political, of who has authority to make policies and shape lives. For example, claiming that women can be politically significant actors has historically been an important part of emancipating women from discriminatory practices.

These last sentences open up two important questions. The first question concerns the inclusion or exclusion of subordinated people in democratic political communities. Who is or can be a citizen of a political community? How does including or excluding groups of people from citizenship change over time? I will come back to this in Chapter 4.

The second question concerns how analysing politics itself asserts values. Different approaches value different practices as political. Analysing politics by focusing on the political elite implicitly asserts that the allocation of values is a top-down process. It reiterates a concept of politics that silences the importance of social movements and ordinary people. Also, this book includes certain judgements about what is political and what is not, about who is a political actor and who is not. One of its purposes is to widen the understanding of what counts as political to a variety of everyday sites and activities. It therefore highlights what more elitist approaches shade out. It values the political nature of everyday decisions of people, such as filling a shopping basket or which company to work for.

SUMMARY

Who does politics?

Usually I would say politicians. They compete for our votes. They try to convince people generally and their party members that their views on how to improve the economy, on how to encourage racial equality, and on whether or not to go to war, for example, are the best options available.

In this chapter I introduced the idea that many more people participate in politics. In the first instance I pointed out that politicians not only compete with one another – for example, when in opposition they formulate policy proposals that compete with the government's policy – they also compete and debate with other professional actors. I used as an example the judges who made some politically controversial decisions in refugee and asylum cases in the UK at the turn of the century.

I then introduced the people as a political actor. Citizens, opinion poll institutions, social movements and interest groups, such as unions, business organizations and farmer organizations, take part in the political contest of what is in the interest of the whole of society. That means that you are, most likely, also participating in politics in many different ways. When you donate to a charity you are supporting a pressure group with certain interests, for example interests of people who are blind or of those with projects in less developed countries. When you do not vote you might be signalling to politicians that you cannot get excited about what they are doing – which usually seems to bother them! If you take part in a public opinion poll you participate in providing your view on an issue of general importance.

I concluded the chapter by suggesting that everyone participates in politics to some extent. As a result, politics changes from a professional, elite business to an everyday and multifaceted activity in which we are all involved in a variety of ways.

Where does politics happen?

The previous chapter started from a narrow understanding of politics but quickly slipped into a more multifaceted concept of politics. Perhaps some of you are interested in retaining a tighter definition. You may ask whether it would be possible to develop a leaner conception of politics by changing the question from 'Who does politics?' to 'Where does politics happen?' This invites answers that focus on the importance of political institutions. At first sight such an approach indeed promises to offer a more focused understanding of politics. Politics would be what happens in national parliaments, governments and their cabinets, and possibly elections. That sounds pretty straightforward.

It is not that simple, however. Politics does not only take place in national institutions; most countries also have many peripheral political institutions. This raises further questions. For example, what is the relation between political institutions in the UK capital, London, and political institutions in Scotland, Wales and Northern Ireland? How do local councils and national governmental institutions compete and collaborate? These questions introduce extra dimensions and complications within an approach that defines politics on the basis of political institutions.

Despite these complications, those of you who are looking for a more precise definition of politics may find the institutional perspective a good option. However, there is a good chance that at some point someone will ask if these formal political institutions are the only sites of politics. Does politics only exist in places that are specifically designed to be political?

I will support the view that politics can also happen in other, more unusual places. By visiting two places that are not specifically designed for facilitating political activities – a pub and a detention centre – I hope to be able to show that politics can happen everywhere. This does not imply that politics necessarily always happens everywhere. It does imply, however, that I argue against limiting the places of politics to formal political institutions. In my understanding, the concept of a political place is as fuzzy as the concept of a political actor. The refugee question again functions as the empirical political context from which I take my examples.

Let's start with a commonplace event one Friday evening in January 2002.

> [Lucas jumps off the bus. He is walking fast to the pub a bit further down the road. He is late. He was supposed to meet Hannah and Jay at 5 p.m. The pub is not too crowded for a Friday. Hannah and Jay sit at a table in the far right corner.]
>
> *Jay*   You can't be serious! We can't send the Afghan refugees back to Afghanistan.
>
> *Hannah*   Why not? The Taliban have been defeated, and strict Islamic rule is over. The civil war has ended. It's a safe country again. No need for the Afghans to stay here.

Jay   Yeah yeah. That's what the Prime Minister and his great buddy, the American President, want us to believe. But you can't really say that Afghanistan's stable. You'll see in a couple of months' time when it's spring. It's always better to fight in spring than in winter, especially in Afghanistan.

Hannah   You always find a reason to support refugees. Why do you like them so much? I think they're a nuisance. They don't belong here. We've already got enough problems in this country. The NHS doesn't work properly. The railways are a shambles. Schools don't have enough money. Why can't we concentrate on our own problems instead of bringing in even more people?

Jay   Careful – my parents were refugees too you know. Have you ever heard the stories of some of the refugees? Women can't help being women can they? Are you suggesting that Bosnian women should have had a sex change so the Serb and Croat militias wouldn't rape them? They raped men too, by the way. To hide underneath the Eurostar, a few inches from the track, to make it to the UK I would have to be pretty desperate. Do you really think ...

FIGURE 11   Doing politics?

Hannah   What are you suggesting? That we should open the borders for everyone and say: 'Please, come to the land of milk and honey. Take my home, my taxes, my ...'

Lucas   Hi. Sorry I'm late. You're not on about refugees again, are you? What about discussing drinks?

Is a discussion about refugees in a local pub after work on a Friday evening 'doing politics'? Or, does the fact that it happens in a pub make it just an ordinary discussion among friends? Can the pub be a place where politics is done? Maybe, but it is definitely not the place where one usually expects to find it. Let's change the setting of the discussion slightly and see what happens.

[It is Friday evening at 6 p.m. in early February 2002. Lucas Smith, MP for the Labour Party, quickly walks to the Houses of Parliament a bit further down the road. He is late. He is supposed to intervene in a parliamentary debate that started at 5 p.m. As usual Parliament is not too crowded. When he finally takes his seat, Hannah Johnson, MP for the Conservative Party, is discussing the situation of the Afghan refugees with Jay Rushdie, MP for the Liberal Democrats.]

Jay Rushdie   The honourable member can't be serious! I firmly believe that it would be irresponsible to send Afghan refugees back to Afghanistan before political, social and economic stability has been guaranteed for a longer period of time.

Hannah Johnson   As the honourable member surely knows the Taliban regime has been defeated. The strict Islamic rule they imposed is over. The civil war has ended. Afghanistan is again a safe country. I can't honestly see a reason, Madame Speaker, why Afghan refugees can't return to their country as of now. Their country needs them.

...

This is definitely a political debate. Changing the characters into Members of Parliament and relocating the discussion to the House of Commons changes the chat between Hannah and Jay from an after-work talk to something that is immediately recognizable as a political debate. One of the reasons is that debates in Parliament more directly bear upon the public contest of values and governmental instruments such as taxes. It is part of the central structure of governance of a state while a pub or canteen is not. Therefore, under normal circumstances places such as Parliament are politically more powerful than a pub or a factory canteen.

While Parliament is obviously a place where politics happens, for me the more interesting question is whether a pub, a factory, a prison, or any other place can be a site of politics too. In the search for an answer, let's leave

'The House will be glad to hear that after much deliberation and discussion this government has made a firm decision — heads we go, tails we don't ...'

Hannah, Lucas and Jay to their drinks for a while and travel to Woomera. Woomera is a small town surrounded by desert in a remote area in the far north of South Australia, 1120 miles west of Sydney. The UK and Australian governments established it in 1946 as a long-range weapons research facility. At the beginning of the twenty-first century it is very much at the periphery, far removed from Australia's political centre. However, in January 2002, Woomera was all over the news. It was not because of a successful rocket launch or a breakthrough in weapon development but because more than 200, mostly Afghan, refugees detained in the detention centre at Woomera went on hunger strike. Some had sewn their lips together, others threatened to commit suicide by jumping onto razor wire, and still others had swallowed potentially lethal cocktails of shampoo and detergents. They protested at the suspension of the processing of their asylum claims, the harsh living conditions in the centre, and the long time – up to three years – it takes for the Australian government to process their application for asylum.

FIGURE 12   Woomera detention centre, January 2002: a detainee stands next to the razor wire fence before jumping and seriously injuring himself

In some ways, a detention centre is an administrative place, just like transit areas in airports where one queues up to show one's passport before entering a country. It usually detains refugees who enter a country illegally for the period it takes to process their asylum application. In that sense the detention centre in Woomera can be interpreted as a kind of waiting room in which people 'queue up' to receive benefits or services from the state. So how did the detention centre become a highly political place in January 2002? How did a 'waiting room' come to be swarmed over by the international media? To some extent this question is similar to asking whether your local health centre would become a political site if you started protesting at the long waiting lists in hospitals while waiting to see your GP.

One way of answering the question is to focus on the dramatic protest of the refugees who were detained in the detention centre. When they went on hunger strike, sewed their lips together and threatened to commit suicide the refugees changed from people passively waiting for their asylum applications to be dealt with into active, dissenting voices challenging the way they were treated. In doing so, they questioned Australia's refugee policy, which uses mandatory detention in an effort to deter asylum seekers from entering the country illegally. John Howard, Australia's Prime Minister at the time said: 'Mandatory detention is part of the process of sending a signal to the world that you cannot come to this country illegally' (quoted in Barkham, 2002).

Similar dissent had happened in other detention centres before. Like in Woomera, administrative centres became spaces where ordinary people challenged local and national policies. However, while Woomera succeeded in attracting national and international media attention and in mobilizing national and international groups in support of its cause, previous protests had been kept relatively quiet. Woomera also stood out because it quickly became an important symbol in the struggle against Australia's refugee policy under Prime Minister John Howard's government. What had happened? How was Woomera transformed, so dramatically and quickly, from a forgotten peripheral place in the desert into a symbol of Australia's refugee policy that dominated the political agenda for a short while?

To understand how this intense politicization of the detention centre in Woomera happened we have to move back in time. In August 2001, Australia was in the middle of a national electoral campaign. On 10 November the electorate was going to decide if the conservative coalition government led by John Howard could have a third term in office. In the middle of its fight for a third term, the government decided to deny entry to a Norwegian freighter with 430 refugees, mainly Afghans, on board, who had been rescued from a sinking boat. After days of trying to convince the captain to sail to another country, the Australian government used the navy to board the ship and transfer the refugees to detention centres in neighbouring Pacific islands. The national and international media intensively covered the crisis. The question of boat-borne refugees became a major electoral issue. Two months later the electorate voted Howard and his coalition back into power for the third successive time. The hardline stance on the issue of refugees played an important role in securing this electoral victory. It also made refugee policy both nationally and internationally a highly visible political issue.

FIGURE 13 The Australian army patrols the waters near the Norwegian ship *Tampa* off the coast of Christmas Island, September 2001

In a sense the political scene was ripe for turning a spectacular protest in a detention centre into a test case for a national and international political struggle over refugee policy. Indeed, the Woomera protest was quickly picked up by social movements. Shortly after the hunger strike started, a few thousand people protested in Australia's three major cities against the government's asylum policy. Religious and human rights groups asserted their political importance by accusing the Australian government of running a concentration camp for asylum seekers. Refugees in other detention centres started protesting too. New groups supporting refugees sprang up in the wake of the Woomera protests. In addition, the Labor Party – the main opposition party – ended its silence on the government's refugee policy in order to position itself as a more critical opposition party. International agencies put the Australian government under pressure. The United Nations High Commissioner for Refugees urged Australia to review its policy of detaining asylum seekers. The government first denied Mary Robinson, the United Nations High Commissioner for Human Rights, access to Woomera. However, it had to change its decision under domestic and international pressure.

Supporters of the refugees were not the only ones to become mobilized. The government and supporters of its refugee policy also tried to get their message to the people and the international community. For example, an opinion published in the Australian newspaper the *Herald Sun* on 31 January 2002

FIGURE 14   Support for John Howard at his Benalong electorate office, October 2001

strongly supported the government's position on the Woomera protest: 'Giving in to asylum seekers who sew their lips simply puts more lives at risk. ... We face a new terrorism, a new threat to reason and democracy: do what I say or this child will be hurt' (Bolt, 2002).

FIGURE 15   Police guard the fence as protestors circle the Woomera detention centre, March 2002

As a result of these and other actions and against the background of a few months of hardline governmental policy, a peripheral detention facility in Woomera was transformed into a highly political place at the centre of national and international politics. It became a symbolic place that played an important role in political contestation over refugee policy in Australia. The protest of the refugees in Woomera played an important role in linking the Woomera detention centre to national and international political contests of power and values. However, the refugees did not do this by themselves. They depended to a considerable extent on what had happened before and on how the protest was picked up by other political actors in Australia and the rest of the world. (In April 2003, the detention centre in Woomera was shut after the last six refugees were moved to another centre outside the South Australian town of Port Augusta.)

What does this tell us about politics? The story introduces three important elements that explain why the detention centre was a political place. First, the protest by the refugees and the support or opposition it triggered made Woomera *a site in which power and values were contested.* In the months preceding the Woomera uprising, refugees had become a stake in the struggle for power among Australia's political elite. The media extensively covered refugee issues while increasing dissatisfaction with the governmental policy among some social movements and non-governmental organizations had made the time ripe to mobilize for a more liberal Australian refugee policy. As a result, the local protest in Woomera became an element in the power struggle between political parties and in a wider national, and international, debate about a conflict of values between sovereign rights of states and humanitarian needs of refugees.

The second important element of the story is that the local power struggle of the refugees and its media coverage *made the conflict of values and the power struggle visible to a wider range of political actors.* Against the electoral and international background, the dramatic protest in Woomera was easily picked up by the media. The dramatic nature of the protest (self-mutilation) facilitated mobilization of support by local, national and international groups that were critical of the government's policy.

Third, the Woomera story shows that the political significance of a place is not decided in advance. *The political importance of certain events and places depends on a number of contingent and subjective factors.* Woomera became a prominent political place of local, national and international significance partly because of the protest of the refugees, the media coverage, the reaction of the government, the mobilization of social movements, international protest and expressions of support for the government. The political power of the hunger strike in Woomera also depended to a considerable extent on events which happened in previous months and which did not in themselves concern the specific conditions of the Woomera detention centre. The political leverage of Woomera also increased because it became intertwined with other political issues. One of the most outspoken of these was the struggle for press freedom. National and international media quickly homed in on the protest in Woomera to highlight some of the unpleasant consequences of Australia's refugee policy. At the same time, the government tried to limit media reporting by denying journalists access to the centre. Paradoxically, this made the case even more interesting for the media. At that point Woomera was not only a catchy event that invited a discussion of Australia's refugee policy through dramatic headlines and images, which would guarantee public attention. The restrictive media policy of the government made the detention centre into a case where the media struggled for the right of independent media coverage and the right to keep the public informed.

Because Woomera was such a high-profile case its political significance is easy to grasp. However, if politics is about power struggle and conflicting values, an important question arises. Would you consider the Woomera detention centre a political space if the protest of the refugees had not been covered extensively by the media and if it had not triggered a political struggle between supporters and opponents of government refugee policies in Australia? In other words, would Woomera still be a political place if the protest was limited to a contest of power and values between the authorities running the detention centre and the refugees?

This chapter is drawing to a close. Let's go back to the pub briefly. In our initial story we left Jay, Hannah and Lucas when they were ordering drinks. While we spent time looking at the protests in the detention centre in Woomera, they continued discussing UK refugee policy for a short while, but soon they moved to the latest gossip from work. The following day Jay picks up a leaflet announcing a protest march against the government's refugee policy. She decides to join in. Some time later, Lucas finds himself in a polling station ready to cast his vote. He shared Hannah's opinion in the pub discussion. He decides to vote for the party with the toughest stance on refugee issues. Hannah in the meantime has changed her mind and decides that the UK would benefit from accepting refugees. So, she casts a vote for a more liberal refugee policy. If this were indeed the conclusion of the story, would this have made the pub more unambiguously a place of politics? Can a place of entertainment and leisure ever be a site where ordinary people do politics? Or, is it rather the kind of people, their actions and the debates they endorse which make places such as a bookshop, a theatre or a factory political?

I have noted earlier that politics can happen in each of these sites but not necessarily all the time. The question of what makes a particular place a site of politics thus invites further questions about who can do politics, what makes political practice different from leisure, caring or economic practices, and so on.

The examples of the pub and the detention centre, however, do not simply leave us with yet more questions. They give us some important elements of how a place that is not a formal political institution can become a site of politics. The detention centre in Woomera was political because the protest succeeded with the help of the media, social movements, and the main opposition party, among others, in connecting the private demands of the refugees to the universal right of protection expressed in the Geneva Convention and to a more general debate about the values that underpin Australia's political identity. The private discussion in the pub acquired political dimensions when it influenced how the participants developed their ideas about which principles and interests should prevail in UK politics. They expressed their choices by participating in protest marches and by voting for candidates that they saw as supporting these particular principles and interests. A place thus transforms into a political site when the contest of power bears upon values and interests that are significant for the wider political community. In more general terms, this means that activities in the private sphere – for example discussions in a pub, a factory canteen or a family home – are political when they bear upon interests and values in the public sphere – for example via voting, protesting or petitioning.

However, the private pub discussion is also political in a different sense. The different views of Hannah and Jay reflect different positions and values – such as multiculturalism, protection of human dignity, or priority of wealth of national citizens – which underpin and structure the public political debate. In other words, their discussion in the private sphere mirrors a public contest of values and thus reflects the terms of an important political debate. Hannah represents the opinion that increasing and maintaining levels of wealth of nationals should prevail over protecting refugees. Jay represents the opinion that people have a fundamental right to be protected against persecution which must be given priority over other concerns. In this understanding, the private sphere is political, but not because it helps people to formulate or change their opinion which they subsequently express publicly. The important point is that the private sphere is political because in so far as politics is a contest of values it reproduces in everyday activities the values that underpin different political positions. It closes off certain political positions, possible in principle but not in practice, and makes others readily available. Supporting concentration camps aimed at eliminating refugees or immigrants is not a readily available option in debates about refugees, for example. There are many reasons why this is the case; one of them is that such an extreme expression of twisted nationalism has been deeply discredited in Europe. This view also implies that if this option frequently emerges again in private discussions it may indicate that a discredited policy is being re-introduced into the contest of values in a society. It becomes again a subject of discussion and thus a position that one can gradually try to express publicly.

I conclude this chapter with another question that follows from the discussion about the nature of political sites. If the contest of power and values refers to a political community to which the values apply, then what is the relevant political community? Sometimes the definition of what is the relevant political community is part of the political contest itself. For example, in the case of the Woomera detention centre, some claimed that the Australian community was part of the world community of states that had pledged to protect people claiming refugee status in certain ways. The argument was that this universal right that belongs to all human beings should have priority over national concerns. Others claimed that it was not the values and interests of the world community that counted most but rather those of the national community. I raise this issue because it demonstrates that politics is not just about the contest of power and values within a community. Such a definition leaves one very important aspect untouched: which community are we speaking about? The global community of human beings, the European community, the UK community, the Welsh or Scottish community, ... How we define the particular community of people to which politics applies is itself a political practice and is the subject of the next chapter.

Does politics happen everywhere?

Think of an ordinary place (for example a shopping centre, day centre, restaurant, playgroup, private garden or factory canteen) and consider the conditions that could make it a political space.

SUMMARY

Where does politics happen?

The obvious answer is in national and regional parliaments, in governments and in international organizations. These are institutions that have been specifically designed for politics. However, they are not the only places where politics happens.

I argued that politics can happen everywhere but not all the time. In other words, every place can be, but does not necessarily have to be, a political site. I used the protest in the detention centre in Woomera and a pub discussion after work to introduce how an administrative and a private leisure facility can be seen as places of politics. I am sure you can come up with other interesting examples – a street, the Internet, a supermarket. When anti-refugee protesters started attacking refugees in the streets of Dover or when the pro-hunting lobby rallied hundreds of thousands of people in London then traffic had to give way to political activity. Instead of cars and buses, the streets channelled a political struggle. When you decide not to buy organic products or to boycott products that contain genetically modified ingredients you make your supermarket into a political site.

If I open up the definition of political space beyond the traditional political institutions I have to think harder about what it means to be political. While it is common sense that parliamentary debates and European Council meetings are political, this is not the case for shopping in a supermarket, having a discussion over a few pints in a pub or writing an email from home. I emphasized that two elements are necessary for transforming an everyday place into a political site:

- a contest of power and values
- the contest bears upon values and policies that apply to a wider community.

This definition allows us to argue that not all emails are political. When you write to friends to invite them to a party, you do not do politics. However, when you invite them to a political rally of the local Conservative Party or to discuss how to set up neighbourhood schemes to reduce crime your house briefly becomes a political site. It is briefly a place from which you try to mobilize people to participate in a contest of power and values that bears upon a wider community; for example, a neighbourhood or a nation.

Who belongs to a political community?

If politics is a contest of power and values within and between political communities, then the question arises of what is the political community. In this chapter I focus on the political community as an organization with particular procedures and criteria defining who can be a member – that is, a citizen. It also puts a lot of effort into maintaining the loyalty of its members. Often politics concerns the allocation of values, rights and duties to the members of the community (for example, protecting citizens from external aggression or aspiring towards a more equal distribution of wealth among citizens). However, politics is also a contest over the nature of the political community itself. Citizens and politicians contest criteria for membership, for instance. They also contest or support political identification of the members with the community. For example, in time of war patriotic values are consciously played out by politicians and the media. The purpose is to unify citizens behind the political decision and the army.

In this chapter I introduce a few ideas with regard to how the political community is practically realized. I focus on political processes that discriminate between insiders and outsiders. How is membership of political communities created, maintained and changed over time? What are the instruments for including and excluding people?

One way of realizing a political community is through citizenship. Members of the community are given particular rights and entitlements and have certain duties towards the community. For example, citizens of the European Union can vote in local and European elections in their country of residence and in national elections in their country of nationality; citizens of the EU pay less for university fees in the UK than citizens of states that are not members of the EU. Other examples of traditional citizenship rights are entitlement to work and to reside in a country, entitlement to welfare benefits, a duty to pay taxes, etc. Some of these rights and duties are not limited to those citizens who have a right to carry the passport of a particular country. For example, immigrants usually have a right to reside, permission to work and a duty to pay taxes without formally having national citizenship. Indeed, immigrants raise an interesting question about what defines membership of a political community. Do particular rights and duties define membership or does nationality? If it is the former, then citizenship is not an all-or-nothing category. Immigrants enjoy particular rights and have certain duties. They can thus be seen as members of the political community in which they reside. But they may not be citizens to the same extent as nationals are. For example, they may not have a right to vote or a right of permanent residence.

Citizenship thus seems to be related to, but not fully covered by, that other great, modern criterion of political membership: nationality. As nationals, members of a political community not only share particular rights and duties, they are also assumed to share a cultural identity. As a nation, a political community nourishes the sharing of history, traditions, language, religion and/or values. Let me give you a few examples. Political speeches will often refer to the greatness of a country, to the people cherishing the value of democracy, or to the people taking the lead in the fight against violations of human rights. History classes often repeat the idea that the people of a country share traditions and values. Playing the national anthem before important sports events, defending the pound sterling as a currency, or showing the Union flag in news bulletins express the idea of being united in being British.

'You have to admire the way he can play all our national anthems'

The very fact that a nation needs to be affirmed continuously suggests that a nation, and more generally a political community, is something that is politically created and needs to be maintained to prevent it from falling apart. The creation of nationhood often requires an active politics of forgetting some inconvenient elements of one's history. For example, nationalist opponents of immigration and refugees often neglect to mention that they themselves are most likely descendants from migration flows going back as far as the massive movements of tribes in Europe during the creation of the Roman Empire. This view of national identity also implies that the values and traditions that characterize a nation can be contested. In more extreme cases some people will actively resist their membership of a particular nation; for example, Kurds in Turkey and Irish nationalists in Northern Ireland.

FIGURE 16 Mexicans wait to cross the border into the USA, February 1997

Differentiating insiders from outsiders is one of the key elements in forging a political community. Contests of ways of differentiating insiders from outsiders and of regulating inclusion and exclusion are politically important because they affect the way in which people identify with their political community and the way in which they can be mobilized in support of policy decisions. Below I introduce the argument that discrimination between insiders and outsiders and identification with a political community is not limited to a cultural process of nation building. Administrative instruments and everyday discrimination play at least as important a role in forging political community and regulating inclusion and exclusion as do national symbols such as the national anthem, the flag or representations of a shared history.

Early on in this book I introduced a classic example of the regulation of inclusion and exclusion in modern political communities: border controls. When the Austrian military patrolled the border with Hungary to prevent illegal immigrants and refugees from entering Austria, they asserted that Austria is not open to everyone. Policing territorial borders is among the most spectacular measures regulating the inclusion and exclusion of people; just have a look at Figure 16 showing the fence in Southern California at the border with Mexico. However, policing borders is not the only and arguably often not even the most important means for discriminating insiders from outsiders. Many administrative devices in modern states have discriminating effects. They may not be exclusively designed as tools for separating insiders from outsiders but they often function as if they were.

I use an example of an instrument developed in the context of refugee policy to clarify this argument and to illustrate the multidimensional, administrative and everyday nature of the construction of membership of a political community. In working through the nature and functions of a particular, unspectacular administrative instrument I want to bring out how inclusion and exclusion is managed in everyday life and how ordinary people participate in it. The device I look at was politically contested within the UK, which ultimately led to it being withdrawn. It is pictured opposite.

What are they?

They're shopping vouchers.

They're what?

Pieces of paper refugees had to use to pay for their grocery shopping in supermarkets in the UK from late 1999 until April 2002.

Vouchers were introduced in the Immigration and Asylum Act of 1999. This act made a few changes in asylum policy. It introduced a policy of dispersing refugees within the territory of the UK, to relieve London particularly where a disproportionately high number of asylum applicants resided. The act also removed asylum seekers from the mainstream welfare system, especially Income Support. Grocery vouchers were substituted for cash benefits that would normally be given under Income Support. In 2000, an adult asylum seeker without dependants received £26.54 in vouchers to buy food and clothing and £10 in cash per week. The vouchers could only be spent in specified shops, and no change could be given if the total price of the products required was less than the value of the voucher. The difference went to the shop owner.

The UK was not the only country that removed asylum applicants from the welfare system in the 1990s. Germany and Belgium, for example, did the same. The question which then arises is why would a country substitute vouchers for cash? Does it make a difference whether refugees pay their bills in supermarkets with money or with vouchers? It does, and the best indication of this is that in 2002 the UK government abolished the voucher system, partly as a result of protest by refugee organizations such as the Refugee Council and partly because of general dissatisfaction with the system.

At first sight vouchers functioned like cash income support. They provided asylum seekers with a minimum income that allowed them to buy food and clothing. In other words, it allowed them to survive in the receiving country during the time their asylum application was looked at. In that sense one can argue that vouchers were an instrument of including refugees in everyday life in a community, similar to any kind of income support. In contrast to those held in a detention centre, for example, these refugees could go shopping with the vouchers. But why would a government set up a voucher system, which requires personnel and money to administer it, when the same result could be reached by giving asylum applicants money instead of vouchers?

Vouchers are not like money in one very important respect: they are not anonymous and universal. Money is nameless. It does not identify the person using it in a particular way. It is a generally accepted means to pay for services and goods, irrespective of the status of the person. Not so with vouchers. Vouchers are less flexible. They can only be spent in particular shops. They cannot be used to pay for services, such as translation of documents, which is often required when applying for asylum. They also readily identify a person as a refugee because most other people in the shop pay by credit card or cash.

One of the reasons for setting up the voucher system was to dissuade refugees from coming to the country. Decision makers assumed that refugees are attracted to cash benefits that would provide them with a higher standard of living than in their home country. In other words, cash benefits were seen as a factor attracting economic refugees – who primarily tried to improve their economic situation – rather than political refugees fleeing persecution. Vouchers were seen as an instrument that would provide some level of income support but without having the attraction and flexibility of money.

> As in Britain, the intention behind the support system was to make Germany less attractive to economic migrants at a time when nearly 400,000 refugees each year were seeking a new life in the federal republic. Last year the number fell below 100,000 for the first time since 1993, suggesting that stricter measures have worked. ...
>
> The German equivalent of the legislation now going through Parliament [the Immigration and Asylum Act 1999] is a 1993 law that excluded asylum seekers

from the Federal Social Assistance Act. Benefits in kind replaced cash which, it was claimed, was being used to pay traffickers to smuggle illegal immigrants into Germany.

(Johnston, 1999)

One of the purposes of the voucher system was thus similar to increasing border controls: to make it more difficult or less attractive for refugees to come to the UK. But why does one dissuade refugees from coming to a country? One of the underlying assumptions is that a country first of all has to serve its own national citizens. Refugees do not really belong to the UK. Their home country is elsewhere. Under the Geneva Convention the citizens of the UK have agreed to extend their community to particular categories of refugees – to people fleeing persecution – but not to those fleeing economic hardship.

The key point I want to make here does not directly concern the question of whether the distinction between economic and political refuge is a practical and/or just distinction. Rather, I want to draw attention to the fact that political communities patrol their membership by means of administrative instruments. Besides nurturing national identity, states have developed a number of sophisticated instruments to patrol the boundaries of their political community. Visas, passports, border control, and special registration systems are among the many devices that a state uses to differentiate citizens from non-citizens. Not everyone can enter the UK and those who do arrive usually do not receive the same rights and entitlement as UK citizens.

FIGURE 17   Travellers queue for passport control at Arlanda airport, Stockholm

The voucher system facilitated drawing distinctions between UK citizens and refugees in a much more sophisticated way than by simply deterring refugees from making the move to the UK. It was also a system of identifying and controlling outsiders who had already entered the national territory.

Vouchers had to be collected from a post office. Refugees could shop only in particular stores with the vouchers. How does that relate to identifying and controlling refugees as outsiders? In so far as refugees depended on these vouchers for income support, they limited their freedom of movement within the territory, or, more specifically, within the national consumer market. National citizens, who are full members of the national community, usually enjoy equal freedom of movement within the territory of a liberal democratic state. Nobody really determines where citizens can and cannot shop, for example.

In addition, the post office can track who has collected their vouchers and who has not. Where has refugee Iria gone to since she does not collect her vouchers? How would refugee Atos survive without his vouchers?

Vouchers also facilitate exclusion in very mundane and everyday situations. Let's visit the local supermarket. It is Saturday afternoon, 15 September 2001. I have been queuing at the till for fifteen minutes. Only one family more and then it is my turn. Why does it take so long for them to pay? What are they paying with? It looks like cheques. What are they doing now? Are they taking something out of the trolley? Do they not have enough money? Why did they take so many things in the first place then? Someone behind me whispers: 'Hurry up. I've got other things to do'. The people in front of me are nervously trying to decide which of their items they will return. Then it is finally my turn. The cashier apologizes. 'Sorry about the delay.' The people before me turned out to be refugees paying with vouchers. They cannot receive change so they try to reach a total as close as possible to what they are entitled to.

What does this tell us about the social function of a voucher? It identifies the persons in front of me as being different. They do not pay in the usual way for their shopping. The questions in my mind, the whispering in the queue and the apology of the cashier also demonstrate a feeling of unease towards the refugees. The unease was not a result of their refugee status as such but of the use of an unusual means of paying for their shopping. The vouchers thus demonstrated something unusual and discrediting about the persons using them. In brief, vouchers are a sign that disqualifies persons from full social acceptance. They function like a stigma (Goffman, 1990; first published 1963). They draw a distinction between national citizens and refugees in ordinary situations. The refugees are immediately identified as being different from anyone else in the supermarket, except for other refugees. The reverse side of this is that the 'normal' people who can pay by cash recognize themselves as being together. The queue is suddenly more than a simple line of people waiting to pay for their shopping. They become a group of equals who can recognize themselves as being different from refugees because they equally enjoy the benefit of being able to pay by cash or credit card.

The difference that the vouchers create between those who can pay with money and those who pay with vouchers is political. It asserts who belongs to a particular community (in this case, consumers) and who is at its margins. Of course, refugees are an explicit example of outsiders. They are often citizens of another state who want to enter another community of citizens. However, they are not the only group in the periphery of a society. Homelessness and madness would also be interesting examples of how communities develop instruments of integration and exclusion.

FIGURE 18   A political community?

In making differences visible in everyday life, vouchers can also encourage you to participate in politics. The experience in the supermarket might lead you to write to your local MP asking him or her to abolish the voucher system. Alternatively, it might reinforce your support for those groups who argue that refugees are a nuisance and that they should stay in their own country. By emphasizing the difference between you and the refugee the voucher reaffirms that you belong to a community and that the refugee does not, and by making this explicitly visible it can encourage political activity contesting or asserting institutionalized ways of community building.

Finally, the example demonstrates that inclusion and exclusion from the UK community does not happen exclusively at borders or in UK embassies where diplomats decide whether to give a person a visa. Ordinary people doing their shopping in a local supermarket on a Saturday afternoon can be engaged in practices of inclusion and exclusion as well. A political and administrative decision to introduce vouchers thus created an instrument that made refugees recognizable in everyday situations and facilitated the identification of insiders and outsiders by ordinary people.

I made up the story of the supermarket. However, it is not dissimilar to Sadiq's real experience in a supermarket in north London. Sadiq Hanafi was a refugee from Afghanistan. He was 26 and it took him seven months to make it to London.

> Sadiq is a very private and proud man. He wants to work. After seven months on the road, he arrived exhilarated in London. Now he is frustrated and depressed. His mission to earn money to send back has so far failed. He's still waiting for his first interview with the Home Office. The process of accepting or rejecting his asylum hasn't even begun. In the meantime, he is bewildered by the hatred he sees around him. At a Sainsbury's checkout a few months after he arrived, he was buying food with his £26 worth of grocery vouchers when a voice behind him rasped in his ear. 'Look at you, eating our taxes.' 'I felt so embarrassed at the way she spoke to me but how could I explain?'

(O'Kane, 2001, p.10)

FIGURE 19   Sadiq Hanafi

Sadiq's story adds an important element to the story I have told so far. At first sight, his story just confirms what I said earlier: administrative and political decisions draw boundaries in everyday situations. However, the last sentence adds a new element to the picture. It suggests that something else is going on as well. Sadiq feels embarrassed. Is embarrassment not one of those feelings, such as shame, through which people discredit *themselves*? Does this concluding line suggest that a voucher is a sign that *sticks* to a person and leads to self-exclusion?

The voucher system has the effect of reinforcing a process whereby refugees increasingly identify themselves as outsiders who are not, and perhaps cannot be, 'normal' members of the community. This is a politically relevant effect given the political contest of how to deal with refugees at the time the voucher system was introduced. Vouchers, which at one level are a form of income support and therefore inclusion in a community, are also a sophisticated instrument of exclusion. They identify refugees as outsiders in a twofold way. They combine negative identification of refugees by other citizens with a negative self-identification by refugees reinforcing a self-image of being outsiders.

> I feel we are marked in red because everyone knows that we are refugees when we do our shopping by vouchers. We feel humiliated at the checkout because when we give our vouchers, the cashier's attitude is usually really bad. Usually, when they tell us the total, they won't let us go back to pick up something for the change. ... Other customers who are in the queue behind us ... often look at us in a very bad way, like: 'Look at this asylum seeker, they are here, they are buying things with vouchers and they are holding us up.' We try to be very fast and sometimes we end up making mistakes at the cash desk.
>
> (Gillan, 2001, p.41)

Although this story from a Turkish Kurdish refugee again refers mainly to the exclusionary practice of cashiers and other customers, it also suggests that refugees mark themselves as outsiders. Why try to be quick, even at the cost of making mistakes, when actually you are entitled to use vouchers in a supermarket? Are the other customers looking on 'in a very bad way'? Or are they just curious to find out what is happening? If the latter is the case, refugees may still feel the gaze and translate the looks into exclusionary practices because of their own discomfort with using vouchers. If this interpretation is at least partly correct, it shows how vouchers are quite complicated mechanisms that can nurture practices of self-exclusion among refugees. The Turkish Kurdish family stopped using the vouchers after a while, hence depriving themselves of a source of income.

However, more importantly for our interest is that the family members internalized their refugee identity and the politics surrounding it. The main point is not just the feeling of discomfort that they have when using the vouchers but the reasons why they would feel personal discomfort. One of the reasons seems to be that they have identified themselves within the terms of the political debate: that is, as the unwanted. In line with the dominant negative portrayal in political debates at the time the vouchers were introduced, they understand themselves as persons who do not fully belong to the host country and who the host community would prefer to be somewhere else.

The issue of identity is not just one of personal political identity – namely identifying yourself as an unwanted refugee. It also has an impact on how the Kurdish family relate to members of the host population. By identifying oneself as unwanted one also interprets looks, body movements and sometimes even the mere presence of insiders of a community in a negative way. The curiosity of the latter is often immediately interpreted as an act of exclusion. Imagine moving to a village in which no one uses credit cards. You go to the shop and ask if you can pay by credit card. Some people would look curiously at you: 'Is she intending to pay in plastic?' Some would stare at you. Others would ask you what a credit card is. But you would not necessarily feel excluded. The method of paying could become a topic of conversation between you and some of the other people in the shop. It might be your first step towards getting to know the other people in the village. The situation of the refugee is different. There are good grounds for the refugee family to believe that most of the curiosity is informed by a negative image, irrespective of whether that is indeed the case. The political contest of the refugee question often identified refugees as bogus applicants and largely unwanted people. Within that context it is not difficult to see that the refugee family would interpret the stares and curiosity as exclusionary practices, irrespective of the intent.

I do not want to say that the Kurdish family is responsible for excluding itself. That is not the point. The issue is that the story shows how individuals, including you and me, internalize politics. People feel and act according to categories that have often been shaped by political debates. The story thus shows how the terms of the political debates manifest themselves and are reinforced in the everyday practices of ordinary people. (I made a similar point towards the end of Chapter 3 when explaining how a private discussion in a pub can be political.)

National identity is often constructed powerfully through these rather banal everyday situations. Have you noticed the label 'British beef' in the supermarket? The label is first of all a quality label aimed at helping consumers to identify the quality of the meat. However, during the beef crisis, the same label meant something quite different. For some it still was largely a quality label but now identifying the product as 'possibly dangerous'. For others, however, it meant 'let's buy it to support British farmers' or 'let's buy it because we are British'. In the latter case buying British beef became an expression of national identity. But maybe the political nature of the label is not limited to situations of political crisis. Maybe the label always already functioned, irrespective of the beef crisis, as a latent articulation of national identity. Does it not implicitly play on and sustain national sentiments in relation to activities that we usually would not recognize as community building? Thus, does it not continuously shape our understanding of the world as a world of nations so that we are not surprised when we are asked to choose for or against the nation in moments of crisis?

I dwelt on the example of the quality label because it is important to emphasize that it is not just the Kurdish family that internalizes the terms of political debates, which in the 1990s and in the early years of the twenty-first century tended to identify refugees negatively. Also the people belonging to the host political community act out the different positions of the political contest. Some will be rude to the refugee family. Others may try to support them. Still others will be indifferent. Members of the first two groups will

FIGURE 20   Supporting British meat

indeed have emotional discussions or even a fight over their different ways of treating refugees (see also the discussion between Hannah and Jay in Chapter 3).

A final element is that vouchers, which are an administrative tool, make these emotions visible and consequently make the political debates that take place in Westminster and Brussels a reality in a local supermarket. Suddenly political contests over the correct way of dealing with refugees do not seem to be simply a distant matter anymore. If you and I and the refugee family are susceptible to identifying ourselves along the lines of the political debate then politics is brought home in a very intimate way indeed. Political identity is not limited to party affiliation and voting behaviour. It also exists in the way we identify ourselves according to the categories that political debates make available to us.

Can we conclude from the voucher story that the UK political community is constructed in the supermarket? Or, to put it another way, can shopping be a nation-building activity?

S U M M A R Y

Who belongs to a political community?

Politics takes place between members of political communities. Not everyone is or can be a member of a particular political community.

Usually membership of a political community is discussed in terms of citizenship and/or nationality. However, I decided to focus on a specific administrative instrument to show how differentiating between insiders and outsiders takes place in ordinary situations. I also wanted to show how an instrument, which was an outcome of a political contest over how to limit the number of refugees who enter the UK, has an impact on political identification in a multidimensional way. The voucher reinforces that refugees are outsiders because it excludes them from the common system of income support. Vouchers also make it easy for ordinary people to identify refugees in supermarkets. Moreover, they help refugees to internalize a negative self-image of someone who is a burden and who does not belong.

You may find the example I chose rather exotic or extraordinary. I am sure you must have come across other ways in which political identity is reinforced in everyday situations. Let's take one that comes to my mind right now: lining up for passport control in a major airport terminal in the European Union. If you are a citizen of the EU you will go to the line for nationals of the member states of the EU. If you do not hold a passport of one of the member states you will queue in the line for third-country nationals. You sort yourself into the appropriate queue and therefore express your political identity as EU citizen or third-country national.

Political identity – your belonging to a political community – often manifests itself and is reinforced in a banal way and in ordinary situations. However, we should not forget either that arranging for two different line-ups in major airport terminals was a political decision – an outcome of a contest of power and values – that supports the creation of a European political identity in the EU.

How does one encounter the state?

chapter 5

In this chapter I continue with the question of the nature of political community. In the previous chapter I focused on the political community as a membership organization. Now I develop the idea that a political community is also a powerful governmental structure that allocates benefits, builds infrastructure, secures neighbourhoods, provides public services, etc. The institutions and instruments of statecraft extensively and continuously shape and influence our everyday lives.

In liberal democracies three separate branches of authority govern society: legislative authority (that is, a parliament), executive authority (that is, a government and a civil service) and judicial authority (that is, judges and courts). This authority structure develops, applies and enforces within the limits of the law a wide variety of policies. The fact that many policies are largely obeyed and can be legitimately enforced derives to a considerable extent from the power that is lodged within this governmental structure.

When I moved the dialogue between Hannah and Jay from the pub to Parliament in Chapter 3, the conversation became more recognizably political precisely because it became part of this governmental machine. People operating in this structure are more directly involved in developing the instruments for steering a society in a preferred direction. Vouchers and detention centres are two of the instruments that I have already discussed and that have been used to implement the opinion that refugee flows should be restricted.

In this chapter I unpack a few important elements of this governmental structure by exploring the question 'How do refugees encounter the state?' People come across the state in a wide variety of situations. Every day you interact with your state in a number of ways: using public roads, visiting your doctor, dropping your kids off at a state school in the morning, paying VAT, taking glass and paper to a recycling point, etc. These encounters often do not have an explicit political content. They are, of course, in one way or the other an outcome of political decisions but in themselves they are not necessarily experienced in terms of power and values. We use the facilities, we accept that we have to fill in forms, etc. However, these many facilities and administrative procedures are political. To explain this I will draw in the first instance on examples from the less ordinary yet certainly revealing situations in which refugees encounter the governmental structure of the receiving state. The focus is very much on the UK but many of the issues apply to other countries as well.

Let's start with a sentence taken from the Home Office website that deals with asylum in the UK.

> The UK is a signatory to 1951 UN Convention relating to the Status of Refugees and its 1967 Protocol. All applications for asylum made at UK ports of entry or within the country are considered in accordance with the obligations under the Convention.
>
> (Home Office, 2002a)

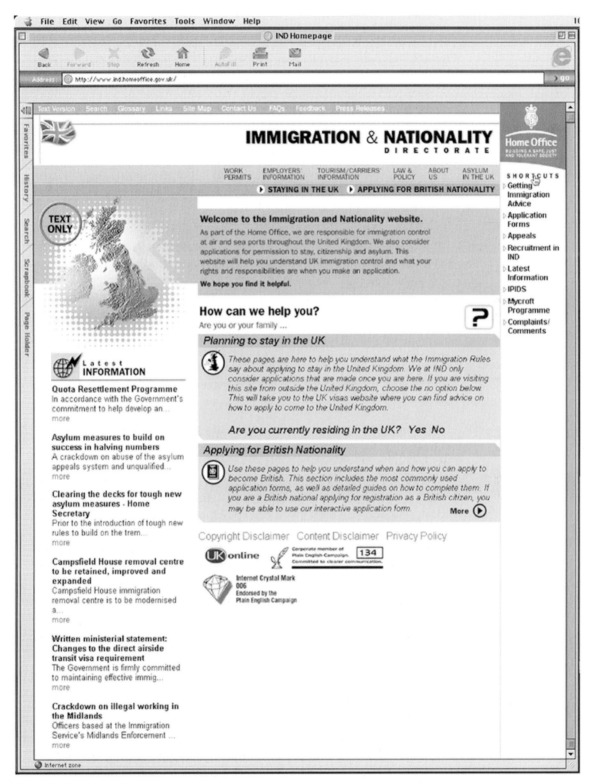

FIGURE 21 An encounter with the state: the UK Home Office, Immigration and Nationality Directorate website

Source: Home Office, 2003

The quotation pictures the state as an entity that applies the law that it has legislated or to which it has subscribed. Refugees encounter the state as rights holders. Similar to citizens, they are subjects who have rights that the state should honour. In the case of the refugee, one of the main rights is the right of protection as defined in the Geneva Convention (see Chapter 2). The idea that citizens and refugees hold rights is generally seen as an important characteristic of liberal democratic government. Some of the most basic rights, such as the right of protection from state persecution, are designed to protect people from arbitrary decisions of a state. Other rights define entitlements which provide opportunities for people; for example, both citizens and refugees can be entitled to health care and education.

Rights have been and continue to be a major subject of politics. Much of the contest of power and values in states is about retaining, changing and/or developing new rights. For example, questions such as whether the Geneva Convention needs to be changed or whether children of refugees should be taught in separate schools until their asylum application has been decided have been subject to fierce political debate.

Focusing on rights tends to present the encounter between state and refugees in legal terms. But refugees do not just encounter the judicial face of the state.

Browsing the Home Office website on asylum, I came across a page entitled 'Asylum applications – a brief guide to procedures in the UK'. This page starts as follows:

MAKING AN APPLICATION

Asylum seekers can make their application at their port of entry to the UK – a 'port' application – or to the Immigration and Nationality Directorate (IND) if they have already entered the UK – an 'in country' application.

(Home Office, 2002b)

That is almost the same sentence as the final sentence in the previous quotation. It is an important sentence because it introduces the territorial nature of the state. That means that to claim the right of protection refugees have to make it to the territory of another state. How do refugees encounter this territorial face of the state?

Tonight is quiet, and it has gone 3 a.m. when Dante arrives bearing half a mile of wagons from Milan. Anderson [a 54-year-old former funeral director who now checks cargo wagons that enter the UK for stowaways] has reached the last-but-one container when the sporadic beeping of his console accelerates to an insistent chirp. After calling Kent police, he opens the back of the wagon and climbs in, peering behind boxes at a jumble of bodies in the dark. 'Fast asleep,' he says, mostly to himself. 'Can you believe that?'

'Speak English? Hello? English?' says a tiny woman from the Home Office, who has been accompanying Anderson all night but won't tell me her name. 'Where are you from? Kosovo, Turkey, Afghanistan, Palestinian, Albanian?'

(Burkeman, 2001, p.36)

FIGURE 22   Searching for asylum seekers in a freight yard in Folkestone

The important observation that follows from this quotation is that the territory of the UK is not just a geographical given. It is also an instrument for governing refugee flows. Towards the end of the 1990s controlling illegal immigration by increasing border controls was a highly visible and also contested policy in Western Europe (see also Chapter 1). The use of advanced technology such as heat detectors and spectacular stories such as Italian coastguards chasing Albanian people traffickers in the Adriatic Sea made for interesting reporting. The spectacle itself is not what I want to emphasize here, however. The important issue is that the territorial nature of the state becomes a reality for refugees through the various means and people who control and manage unwanted penetration of state territory – and thus of the political community. The means range from passports and visas to high-speed boats and data banks such as Eurodac (Figure 23). The people include customs, police and personnel of private transport companies.

The means to control borders and the movement of people thus makes territory into a political reality. 'Political' refers to different things here. It implies that territory is an instrument of political rule. But it is also political in the sense that it is contested. Wars over territory are among the most radical examples of this. In addition, illegal immigrants contest the territorial integrity

FIGURE 23   Controlling entrance to state territory: US Secretary of State Colin Powell shows a new visa with improved safety features, July 2002; and the Eurodac system for comparison of fingerprints for asylum applicants in the EU

of the UK. Refugees making it to the UK in great numbers contest, too, immigration and refugee policy of the UK government. If refugees still arrive in significant numbers after policies have been developed to dramatically reduce their number, the refugees implicitly question governmental claims that policies will work.

> *You might say*   These are kind of interesting stories. But surely the important question is: what does it actually mean for a refugee to claim a right in a state?
>
> *I could respond*   Yes. For refugees one of the main aspects is applying for asylum.
>
> *You*   Do refugees just shout at the border or in Covent Garden: 'I want asylum!'? How do they really enter a juridical relation with the state?
>
> *I*   Oh, you are after the details?
>
> *You*   Details? To me they seem rather important. Otherwise rights just remain statements, don't they? I guess rights holders do not just want to hold rights but would also want to claim them and use them in practice.
>
> *I*   Alright. Let's go back to the website of the Home Office.

Nine short sections on the website that explain different aspects of the application procedure follow the previously quoted section 'Making an application'. Among others they refer to an asylum screening interview, fast-tracking, evidence about the claim and decisions. Under each of these headings the text explains what seem to be the crucial steps in the application procedure.

Let's look at one of them, 'Decisions'.

DECISIONS

Asylum claims are considered by caseworkers or immigration officers who are specially trained to consider applications in accordance with the 1951 UN Refugees Convention. Each claim is examined individually on its merits. The caseworker must decide whether the facts show a reasonable likelihood of persecution to the asylum seeker for a Convention reason in the event of a return to their country of nationality or habitual residence. To amount to a 'well-founded fear of persecution' a judgement by the Law Lords decided that the fear must be objective. A decision will be made on the basis of the information contained in the SEF, any other documents that have been provided by the applicant in English, and the interview. Caseworkers have access to detailed Country Assessments to assist them when considering the claim. Decisions are notified in writing. The outcome is normally sent by post but in certain circumstances, the applicant may be told of the decision in person.

(Home Office, 2002b)

You might ask   (Bearing in mind what I've previously said in this book about the separation of powers in a democratic state and the rule of law) Where is the judge?

I   There is no judge.

You   What do you mean? There's no judge? Who decides if I qualify for asylum or not? How do I claim my rights?

I   Read the information from the Home Office. It says that a caseworker will decide.

You   Who is that?

I   A caseworker is a civil servant trained to deal with asylum applications.

   ...

You   What is an SEF?

I   That is the document 'Statement of Evidence Form' which refugees usually receive after reporting to immigration officers. It contains approximately 120 questions in 19 A4 pages. In answering them asylum seekers detail why they are seeking asylum. The form has to be filled in within 14 days and in English. If the form does not reach the appropriate authorities within 14 days, the application will be refused.

   ...

We could go on detailing people, procedures and forms. However, this is not a book on how to apply for asylum. I am primarily interested in the governmental structure of the state.

The procedures above show a very familiar face of the state: the bureaucracy. Once at a port of entry or within the territory asylum applicants enter a detailed administrative procedure. Making a right or entitlement into an effective claim often involves engaging with the administrative face of the state. Refugees will have to follow particular formalized procedures to be able to effectively claim asylum, such as filling in an SEF in time.

FIGURE 24 Lunar House, Croydon, home of the UK government immigration centre

In the name of efficiency and objectivity many countries have developed a formal administrative procedure that in principle treats all applicants equally. Standard forms have to be filled in. Asylum applicants have to move through a formalized sequence of stages. Professionals who are specifically trained for their tasks implement each of these stages. An asylum application sets a rationalizing machinery in motion that is designed to process asylum seekers as effectively and equally as possible.

Frustration with civil servants is often the result of having to follow standardized procedures such as filling in forms and of the depersonalized service that one receives. However, it has to be said that these procedures enable equal treatment of different applicants: they all have to follow the same procedure and fill in the same forms. They also depersonalize the relation between asylum seekers and civil servants which should limit favouritism. Although bureaucratic procedures may not work in a very humane way, they enable the state, at least in principle, to treat asylum applicants equally. Equality refers here to treating people according to the same procedures, irrespective of their specific status or characteristics.

'Now will you believe I've been on a two-week holiday in Majorca?'

In addition, I need to mention that modern bureaucracy has made it possible for modern states to govern an extensive range of policy areas – education, work relations, marriage, childcare, pensions, health, etc. – and thus to shape many important aspects of everyday life for millions of individuals. Whether this is for better or for worse is a question of opinion! For example, if a government concludes that it cannot grant asylum to everyone requesting it, it needs a mechanism to determine who are, and who are not, refugees in terms of the Geneva Convention. The asylum procedure, the forms and the civil servants institutionalize a mechanism for distinguishing political refugees (in terms of the Convention) from economic ones.

At this point you could ask: 'Where is the politics? Where is the contest of power and values in the bureaucratic practices?'

These questions raise an important theme. Bureaucratic procedures are often seen as taking politics out of the picture or, in more technical terms, as depoliticizing. The forms and procedures are meant to make applying for asylum a standardized practice that eliminates the contest of power and values as much as possible from the process.

'But are the procedures that the refugees encounter not an institutional application of political decisions? Are they not an outcome of politics?' I agree, they are not unconnected to politics; however, one could argue that they are not political themselves. Refugees can contest the policy as much as they want but they will usually have to go through the procedures if they want to obtain asylum. The political decision to have a procedure to allow the administration to make a distinction between economic and political refugees has been made elsewhere and cannot be questioned from within the procedures themselves. The refugee is like a client who wants to buy a service. The forms that need to be filled in, the stages that need to be followed, the specific rights and duties that come with the 'product' of asylum were defined before and elsewhere. You can argue with the cashier in your local swimming pool that entrance should be free for everyone or that one should allow swimming fully dressed, but if you do not pay or do not get into your swimming gear you will not get the service. To politicize the issue you would have to organize a protest, a lobby group, or speak to your local MP. In this understanding, politics takes place in parliament, in protest groups, in lobbying, via a ballot box, etc., but not in the application of administrative procedures itself (see also the example of the Woomera protest in Chapter 3).

Depoliticizing particular practices is not necessarily a bad thing. Would you want your income support, education or your health care to depend on your political opinion or religious allegiances, for example? The depoliticized nature of particular practices enables, at least in principle, an equal and correct application of policies.

This image of the un-political nature of bureaucratic practice does not fully fit reality, however. The contest of power and values does take place within bureaucracies and through administrative procedures. Let me give two examples.

When Germany, France and the Benelux countries decided to work out a way of abolishing their border controls, civil servants started protesting. The so-called Schengen agreements were fiercely opposed by customs, for example. Jobs would be lost and their budgets would shrink considerably when border controls were no longer deemed necessary. If the depoliticizing nature of bureaucracy holds water, protest by customs would be awkward. They are protesting a decision made by elected politicians. On what grounds can they legitimately object to these changes and lobby politicians? Many people might think that civil servants are not involved in contests of power and values but in fact they often are. Bureaucratic units do have their own interests and values that they wish to defend. This often leads to resistance to political decisions, to attempts to influence decisions and to a power struggle between different bureaucratic units. In this sense, bureaucratic units do act politically

The second example is about how the so-called clients of bureaucracies – that is, you, me and the refugees – can contest policy decisions within the bureaucratic procedures. Some refugees will shred their identity papers on entering a country. If that country has a so-called safe-country policy, which implies that if refugees come from a country that is deemed safe then they will be sent back immediately, it makes sense for refugees to destroy their identity papers. Destroying identity papers becomes a political practice that contests the safe-country policy by making it difficult for the administration to apply the policy. Instead of being sent back, refugees will be allowed to enter an asylum application procedure in which one tries to establish first of all their national identity. Then the government could decide to toughen procedures when refugees do not carry proper identity papers. In this context, shredding identity papers is a contest of power and values between refugees on the one hand and the government and its administrators on the other.

Why do I discuss the role and nature of bureaucracy so extensively? I want to show that governing a country – that is, public authorities allocating values, rights and duties – cannot be limited to law making and legal practice. Once you take a more detailed look at how rights and duties are exercised in practice, you will quickly encounter the powerful administrative nature of modern states. Although developing law remains an important political activity, our everyday lives are shaped more directly by administrative processes that turn political decisions into applicable procedures and forms. Given the importance of administrative methods for the modern political community and given the understanding that these methods are meant to be apolitical, it is imperative to raise at least a few questions about how bureaucratic practice can be interpreted as a contest of power and values, that is, as a political practice.

In a way it would be interesting to return now to the story about administrative encounters between the state and refugees. For instance, the appeal procedure or intervention from the Home Secretary in decisions about the removal of an asylum seeker whose application was refused would provide interesting examples of how judicial procedures and political acts are sometimes still the final check on the administrative process. It would make for an interesting story about how the different faces of the state relate to one another. It would show how the authoritative governmental structure that we often call the state consists of different substructures each sustaining specific governing jobs.

In conclusion, the purpose of this chapter was to give you an idea about how people encounter the state and how this encounter is political. The different stories show how a political community is not only present in people's lives in the form of the national anthem, as the land one walks on, or as the national football team. It is also a highly sophisticated and very powerful governmental structure that shapes many dimensions of people's everyday lives. One of the interesting aspects of the modern political community is that most citizens

FIGURE 25   The presence of the state?

most of the time do not realize that they engage with their state. Many of the encounters are extremely well integrated in everyday life. Who considers dropping off children at school as an encounter with the state?

How would you recognize the presence of the state? What would you look for? A satellite picture of your country? The law section in the national library? A ballot form? The playground in your local park? Your passport? Your doctor? The national flag?

SUMMARY

How does one encounter the state?

Political community is not just about political identity and membership. It is also a governmental entity that allocates values, rights and duties. How does one encounter this political machine, often called 'the state'?

A common way of approaching this question is to focus on the rights and duties that are inscribed in the law. It is through national law that the state presents itself to people. I argued, however, that the modern state is also an administrative entity. It pervades everyday life through forms that need to be filled in, through maintaining national and local infrastructure, through procedures that one needs to follow to obtain a driving licence, through handing out passports, etc. The administrative nature of the allocation of values, rights and duties translates the abstract notion of the state into an everyday reality. We have become so used to the omnipresent nature of the administrative state and its politics that we often do not realize its presence.

Both the extent to which the state should shape different aspects of everyday life and the methods it uses to do this are the subject of much of contemporary political debate. When the Labour government in the UK was discussing the introduction of university fees, it was contesting the idea that the best way to democratize university degrees is free access to university education for everyone who qualifies. It was also contesting the idea that university education is a public good that contributes to the general welfare in a society. It presented university education much more in market terms as a personal investment by the student in the hope of gaining (financial) returns in the form of higher wages. When parents decide not to encourage their children to go to university because it is too expensive, or when potential students decide that paying fees does not matter that much and still go to university, they are actively participating in politics through their private decisions. They participate in the contest of the procedures and nature of university education. Politics seems to be, once again, more multifaceted and more present in our lives than we usually think.

Conclusion

In this book I have emphasized the breadth and multifaceted nature of political practice. I illustrated the point that politics takes place in unexpected places and that it involves a wide variety of people and activities. I also showed that politics is not necessarily something removed from our ordinary lives but that it pervades everyday situations and activities. Therefore, the underlying argument of the book is that politics is something that cannot be avoided. We are obviously affected by political decisions. We are also actively involved in politics, willingly or unwillingly. We use and get used to public services, we make choices when shopping, we cross borders showing our passports, we vote or we do not vote, we support charities which sometimes are also pressure groups, etc.

One of the consequences of focusing on the richness and the multidimensional nature of politics is that I cannot give you a simple answer to the question 'What is politics?' However, like Michelle suggested in the introduction, that could well be one of the main reasons why studying and doing politics can be extremely interesting and rewarding. Who wants to study a subject that can be summarized in a few lines anyway?

The book started from the idea that it is more useful and interesting to keep the question 'What is politics?' as open as possible. It enables us to bring to the fore and explore the multiple sides and sites of politics. However, this has not prevented the analysis in this book from using a few general ideas of what makes all these sites and practices political sightings. More specifically, three ideas informed the illustrations and arguments of this book:

- Politics is an activity that defines which problems are important for a society and how these problems are understood within a society. In other words, politics defines both the problems that matter for a society – are refugees a problem? – and the nature of the problems – are refugees threatening society or are they a gain to society?

- Politics is a contest of power and values in public. Politics is thus about conflict between different opinions on what the important issues are for a community and on how to deal with them. The conflict is also about gaining power to implement one's opinion. The contest bears upon what matters publicly, that is its outcome matters not just for the immediate participants in the contest but for a wider range of people in the community. However, many private decisions and activities are also political through their – often implicit – relation to public contests.

- Politics is the authoritative allocation of values, rights and duties for the community as a whole. Politics is not just a contest but also governmental activity in which values, rights and duties are allocated. This concept emphasizes that politics is not just about struggle for power and between opinions but it is also the activity of a governmental machine.

The breadth of politics and its importance can be brought out in different ways. In the stories that I developed I usually started from the more familiar answer to the question of each chapter. I then contrasted it with one or two situations or stories that made politics more unusual. Paradoxically, in each of the cases it turned out that the latter more unfamiliar sides of politics were actually very familiar. They brought politics home, in the sense that they showed how politics happens in and bears upon everyday situations and ordinary practices in which we all participate.

References

Achiron, M. (2003) *A 'Timeless' Treaty Under Attack*, www.unhcr.ch/1951convention/timeless.html and www.unhcr.ch/1951convention/dev-protect02.html (accessed May 2003).

Barkham, P. (2002) 'PM calls asylum protest blackmail', *The Guardian*, 26 January.

Bates, S. (2000) 'Catholic bishops attack "emotive" asylum language', *The Guardian*, 5 May.

Blair, T. (2001) 'Immigrants are seeking asylum in outdated law. The UN Convention governing the treatment of refugees must be reformed', *The Times*, 4 May.

Bolt, A. (2002) 'They must not win', *Herald Sun*, 31 January, p.21.

Burkeman, O. (2001) 'The frontline' in *Welcome to Britain. A Special Investigation into Asylum and Immigration, The Guardian*, June, pp.36–9.

Clarke, M. (2000) 'At breaking point; asylum seekers to flood villages hit by crime and drug addiction', *Daily Mail*, 15 July.

Dyer, C. (2001) 'Are we a soft touch?' in *Welcome to Britain. A Special Investigation into Asylum and Immigration, The Guardian*, June, pp.48–9.

Gillan, A. (2001) 'That won't do nicely' in *Welcome to Britain. A Special Investigation into Asylum and Immigration, The Guardian*, June, pp.40–2.

Goffman, E. (1990; first published 1963) *Stigma. Notes on the Management of Spoiled Identity*, London, Penguin.

Goodwin-Gill, G. (1996) *The Refugee in International Law* (2nd edn), Oxford, Oxford University Press.

Hague, W. (2000) 'Common sense on asylum seekers', *Guardian Unlimited*, 18 April, www.guardian.co.uk/Refugees_in_Britain/Story/0,2763,211679,00.html (accessed March 2002).

Hoffer, P. (1990) 'Austrian soldiers stem refugee tide', *The Daily Telegraph*, 5 September.

Home Office (2002a) 'Asylum in the UK. Fairer, faster and firmer – an introduction to the UK asylum system', Immigration and Nationality Directorate, http://194.203.40.90/default.asp?PageId=15 (accessed April 2002).

Home Office (2002b) 'Asylum in the UK. Asylum applications – a brief guide to procedures in the UK', Immigration and Nationality Directorate, http://194.203.40.90/default.asp?PageId=87 (accessed April 2002).

Home Office (2003) Immigration and Nationality Directorate, http://www.ind.homeoffice.gov.uk/ (accessed October 2003).

Johnston, P. (1999) 'Tough German refugee reform stems the tide', *The Daily Telegraph*, 22 June.

Johnston, P. (2001) 'Migrant fines for hauliers ruled unlawful', *The Daily Telegraph*, 6 December.

Kadare, I. (1991) 'Uprootings that sow seeds of war', *The Guardian*, 13 June.

O'Kane, M. (2001) 'Sadiq's story' in *Welcome to Britain. A Special Investigation into Asylum and Immigration, The Guardian*, June, pp.4–10.

Travis, A. (2001a) 'Migrants ruling angers Blunkett', *The Guardian*, 6 December.

Travis, A. (2001b) 'The way we see it ...' in *Welcome to Britain. A Special Investigation into Asylum and Immigration, The Guardian*, June, pp.12–15.

Traynor, I. (1990) 'The new walls go up', *The Guardian*, 9 November.

UN Convention relating to the Status of Refugees (1951) Geneva, United Nations.

UNHCR (2001) *Asylum Applications in Industrialized Countries: 1980–1999*, Geneva, United Nations High Commissioner for Refugees.

UNHCR (2002) *Statistical Yearbook 2001*, Geneva, United Nations High Commissioner for Refugees.

Acknowledgements

Grateful acknowledgement is made to the following sources for permission to reproduce material in this book.

Figures

Figure 1: © 2001 Heiko Burkhardt; Figures 2, 13, 15 and 16: © Associated Press; Figure 3: © Pierre Perrin/Corbis; Figure 5: © ARNI/UN Archives/1951; Figure 6 (left): © Terry Moore; Figure 6 (right): © Rex Features; Figure 7: © Louvre, Paris/The Bridgeman Art Library; Figure 8: *Welcome to Britain. A Special Investigation into Asylum and Immigration, The Guardian*/G2, 7 June 2001. © ICM Research and *The Guardian*; Figure 9: © Jess Hurd/ Report Digital; Figures 11, 20, 23 (right) and 24: © Rex Features; Figures 12, 17 and 23 (left): PA Photos/EPA; Figure 14: © NewsPix; Figure 19: © Fiona Lloyd-Davies; Figure 21: www.ind.homeoffice.gov.uk, Immigration and Nationality Directorate home page. Crown copyright material is reproduced under Class Licence Number C01W0000065 with the permission of the Controller of HMSO and the Queen's Printer for Scotland; Figure 22: © Duncan Phillips; Figure 25 (top right): © Worldsat Productions/NRSC/ Science Photo Library; Figure 25 (bottom right): © 2002 Crown copyright.

Illustrations

p.8: © Garland/*Daily Telegraph*. Centre for the Study of Cartoons and Caricature, University of Kent at Canterbury; p.34: © Stan McMurty/Atlantic Syndication. Centre for the Study of Cartoons and Caricature, University of Kent at Canterbury; p.47: © Charles Griffin/The Express. Centre for the Study of Cartoons and Caricature, University of Kent at Canterbury; p.67: © Raymond Jackson/Atlantic Syndication. Centre for the Study of Cartoons and Caricature, University of Kent at Canterbury.

Photo p.49: © *The Guardian*.

Cover

Image copyright © PhotoDisc, Inc.

Index